LIFE'S POTHOLES

Moral And Character Issues

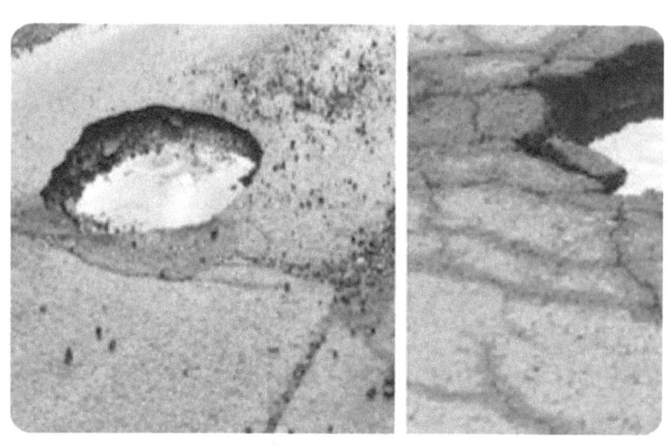

Ben Okorie

GADOL TECH.
CONSULT

Scripture quotations, are taken from the *King James Authorized Version (Old King James) (KJV) and The New Living Translation (NLT)*. Where otherwise, it is stated and indicated.

Partake To Connect The Power In The Holy Communion.

A spirit inspired resource to prepare and discipline the mind for outstanding success-God's Way.

ISBN: 978-978-781-961-6

Publish by GADOL TECH CONSULT

In association with:

SALVATION ASSURANCE & LIBERATION TABERNACLE (SALT) An Outreach Ministry of Ben Okorie and family.

Email: bcokoriegreat@gmail.com

Printed in Nigeria.

DEDICATION

This divine project is dedicated to God the Father, God the Son, and God the Holy Spirit as always to Whom I owe the gratitude in the Communion of grace and truth

AND

The Church, the body of Christ to which I belong, and with which I am in a Communion of fellowship to worship the King of kings.

Let's keep partaking in full measure and wisdom, until He returns to receive us unto Himself.

CONTENT
Page

- Government & Corporate Bodies

5. The Dynamics of Sin And

   Unrighteousness & Obedience in
   Righteousness
6. The Dynamics of Sin And

   Unrighteousness & Obidience in

   Righteousness (II)
7. The Reign of Evil on Earth through

   Lies - the Father And Mother of Potholes

8. Execution of God's Righteous
   Judgment on Sin.

9. A New World Emerged

   After Judgment Events.

10. Pothole Resurfaces

    Post Diluvian Events.

11. Resurfaced Pothole, Takes Hold,

    Spreads & Destroys Yet again.

ACKNOWLEDGMENT

The unrelenting help, support and provisions of God the Father. God the Son and God the Holy Spirit remain my abiding and abounding grace upon which I draw and rely to run this literary race. Faithful.

While the team remains intact and supportive, special mention is hereby made of:

1. EMMANUEL NWANKWO: a friend and editor extraordinary, whose commitment to ensure quality contents and contexts, is unparalleled. Thanks Emma.

2. Emmanuel Agu: The literary keyboardist and technical designer, to shape the thoughts and desires on technical template.

3. Festus Ojukwu: Manager. Gadol Tech, digital planet, Consult and Publications, coordinating and driving the project.

4. Gold Nmesoma Okorie Jesus

My adorable daughter, lead marketer, adviser and finishing director, Overseas 5. Violet Nmema Okorie Jesus

FOREWORD

INSPIRED!

BY THE HOLY SPIRIT AND ADVANCED BY HIM.

BACKGROUND

PITFALLS IN POTHOLES: THE MORAL AND CHARACTER QUESTIONS IN LIFE

Above is a screenshot of Wikipedia's snapshot and post on Potholes. Virtually everyone knows what potholes are. Right there on the road, tarred with asphalt or even on bare laterite soils, it exists.

They exist everywhere, in every country in the world.

Potholes start small most of the time, and as traffic, especially vehicles of various sizes, runs over them, they begin to expand. Then, at a point, if le unfixed, it gets so wide and deep that it poses a great danger to motorists in particular.

The same vehicles that were running over the pothole when it was small and seemingly insignificant begin to avoid it, if they are lucky enough to notice it in good me before they approach it. Otherwise, they bump into it if they are driving at great speed and/or passing that route for the first me. It could be so bad that vehicles can suffer a type burst, tumble, or crash. That's the pitfall dimension of potholes.

That accident could be fatal, not only to the occupants of the vehicle but also to everything and everybody in its vicinity, ranging from pedestrians, animals, markets, culverts, bridges, residential buildings, offices, etc. Nothing around there is safe to the degree of the fatality. There are also the economic and social dimensions and costs of these.

According to Wikipedia, the cause of potholes is undercurrent water, or water dripping on weak asphalt over a long period of me.

When potholes appear in multiples in a particular area, spreading like cancer catching up with other cells, it's an indication that the entire topography of that area is weak. The right course of action in that case is to scrape or excavate the entire area and provide a solid base after solving the problem of the undercurrent and/or dripping water that caused it.

Now, this project is not about road potholes, as could be gleaned from the title. It is rather an allegory for the subject, as told and laid out below.

On June 19th, the Secretary of a popular Town Union in Lagos, Nigeria, in West Africa, operating in a major market located in my area of residence, posted a picture of two potholes on a road, exactly like the one pictured above, on his WhatsApp Status. The footage to the pictures of the potholes reads, "When potholes are small, motorists run over them. When they are big, they avoid them. This post is not about potholes; if you know, you know".

The Town Union is the sponsor, promoter, and owner of an investment project for a shopping mall, with over two hundred lock-up shops, suites, and offices located in a sprawling vast expanse of land within the market.

Then it hit me. I meditated over the post, especially in light of my 2012 investment in the shopping mall, for which this very Secretary has been my contact person. The expected timeline for the completion and allocation of the shops to investors was about 15 months.

At the time of my investment, the president of the association was my contact person until he was deposed. He convinced me to invest in a second shop when I le office in 2014 as a way to adequately supplement my pension. I took his advice and invested in another shop before his removal.

That removal brought me face-to-face with the secretary, whom I understand was the mastermind of that palace coup.

The next thing was that I was told that the cost of the shops had doubled, blaming it on inflation and the cost of things generally.

This was in 2016, two years later I left office. The discordant voices on the actual revised price between the new helmsman and one or two officials I happen to know aroused my curiosity. The real reason for the change of guard began to become clear to me.

Paying another amount, over N1.5 million, into a black hole project that had not materialised five years down the line was neither wise nor rational. I was advised to consolidate the amount I paid for the two shops into one for one shop and have some balance refunded to me since I could not comfortably raise a fresh additional N1.5 million for the two shops.

I did, hoping that the excess amount would be refunded to me immediately after my letter for the consolidation. That was not to be.

All the promises they made to deliver the project in weeks, or at most two months, and every effort I made to achieve exact performance failed.

This is 2023, eleven years after that investment. You can imagine one's state of mind. Pitfall in a pothole!

Based on the pothole post by the Secretary on June 19, 2023, which speaks volumes about his attitude and character causing huge damage to the emotions and health of investors, I sent a WhatsApp message to him the following day, June 20, 2023.

Below is the text of the message, which I also forwarded to another official who had been sympathetic to my case.

A very good morning to you, Sir.
I was privileged to view a very interesting post on your status yesterday.

It was metaphorically about a pothole that began very small and motorists were running over it, only for the same motorists to start avoiding it when, due to lack of due diligence, it was le unfixed, thus expanding to a dangerous size Hmmm!

Isn't it amazing how this parabolic pothole speaks volumes to us as individuals, families, groups, businesses, places of worship, and government because we have taken situations that should have been fixed in good me for granted and allowed them to fester?

That pothole is a metaphor that would, by grace and through the divine power of the one that hears beyond words and sees beyond actions, redound unto those who, by virtue of their positions, power, and actions, have stood on the way of good conscience, what they duly and truly deserve in unfixed relationships across the board.

Great day, sir, and greetings to your family.
Ben Okorie.

Within two minutes of that message that early morning, the Secretary called me on WhatsApp, apologising that the transaction had dragged on for too long. He explained that it's because it's a group thing, in which you have to manage many people and their varying positions and interests on critical issues, adding that it would be a different story if I had transacted with him one-on-one.

He promised for the umpteenth me (one more me, too many in a thousand times in the past, as always) that I could count on his promise on the phone and on my visits in the past, saying: "Oga, oga ebi this month" meaning: "Sir, it would end this month". "Ofoduru publication," meaning it remains a publication. Of what exactly? I don't know.

He had said, "It will end this month," not less than seven times in two years, all to no avail. What they will publish, I don't know.

During my visit in April 2023, he made the same promise, using the word "After Easter," as they were preparing for publication. His kinsman, certainly a member of the association, corroborated the assertion when I reminded him that Easter was in April (a few days away), and he quietly, in a so voice, said, "I know."

Here is the same man, calling me this early morning, begging and re-echoing the same promise he had not kept in years, months, and days. Pothole!

This morning, a day after that interaction in which I told him, I don't have the strength to fight in any sense, heaven would speak. This is because I have lied it to the throne of grace. The Holy Spirit engaged me to write on-The Potholes of Life.

Potholes in health,

Potholes in families,

Potholes in relationships,

Potholes in businesses: faking and cheating

Potholes in addictions-drugs, sex, food and drinks, etc.

Potholes in academics: compromises, low standards, malpractices, sex for marks, producing substandard, ill-equipped graduates

Potholes in ministries: fake prophets and false teachers, impostors, etc. Potholes in construction: substandard materials used in the construction of buildings, roads, rails, bridges, and anything else endangering lives, Potholes in landlord-tenant, patient-doctor, teacher-student, farmer-herder, master servant, etc. relationships

Potholes in governance, corporate and governmental-lack of transparency, accountability, fraud in high and

low places, bribery and corruption, tribalism, nepotism, sexism, feminism, Nazism, etc.
Potholes in international arenas, neocolonialism, wars, racism, etc.

The mother and father of potholes are SIN that began in the Garden of Eden. When our first parents ate of the forbidden fruit, Satan entered into them and through him, sin, and the essence of all sins. Until sin is fixed in man, potholes remain intractable until Christ returns to usher us into a new heaven where the streets are pothole-free but tarred with gold. Even if the question of sin is addressed, there is no pothole-free life here on Earth. We are men with unclean lips. Life can only be managed within the bounds of divine help because the body is not yet redeemed. God, help us live a pothole-patched and spirit-managed life until Christ returns. Amen.

Benjamin Okorie

(Coordinator, Multiply Your Grace-MYG)

CHAPTER 1

TYPES AND SOURCES OF POTHOLES

I know by now we are using pothole as a figure of speech either as simile or allegory. A metaphor that points to something in our lives and relationships both vertically (with God) or horizontally (with ourselves, men, and even our environment) across a broad spectrum of dependent and interdependent engagements.

We are no longer talking about potholes on our roads, but potholes in the expressway of our lives and relationships, and the associated pitfalls of life.

We will draw inspirational truth from the Word of God, the Omnipotent, Omnipresent, and Omniscient. He is Almighty, and in Him lies every strength. He is everywhere at the same me, and He knows all things. Nobody else does it to the degree, finesse, and pedigree he has and demonstrates.

We also draw from contemporary times, based on everyday events.

Types of potholes:

I would, for the sake of simplicity, like to divide potholes into two broad categories.

1. Good potholes and
2. Bad potholes.

1. GOOD POTHOLES:

A good pothole is one that shows up as a sign of an underlying problem that should be examined and addressed before it becomes dangerous. In other words, they begin small, like the conventional road pothole, and if le unfixed on me, they expand and create a big hole that becomes malignant and difficult to manage. The following can therefore be regarded as good potholes:

1. Hunger
2. Anger
3. Pain
4. Conscience (when it accuses, not excuses)
5. Ignorance.
6. Debt.

There are many others.

Based on the binary view, other potholes fall into the category of bad. They are bad not because they are unfixable but because they carry greater danger when they show up and are le unchecked.
We can therefore see the following as:

2. BAD POTHOLES:

1. Lack
2. Poverty
3. Wrath
4. Strife
5. Pride/ arrogance
6. Shame
7. Depression
8. Sickness and death
9. Offence
10. Enslavement
11. Hatred
12. Bitterness
13. Fear
14. anxiety
15. Fraud
16. Bribery and corruption

17. Discrimination (tribalism, racism, nepotism, etc.)
18. SIN GENERALLY (Against God, self, and humanity—stealing, alcoholism, adultery, fornication, addictions to sex, drugs, witchcraft, etc.)
19. 19. Indebtedness
20. Worry.

CHAPTER 2

THE PROGNOSIS OF POTHOLES - GENERALLY

---

16. If you see a Christian brother or sister sinning in a way that does not lead to death, you should pray, and God will give that person life. But there is a sin that leads to death, and I am not saying you should pray for those who commit it.

17. All wicked actions are sin, but not every sin leads to death.
    1 John 5:16-17 NLT.

Potholes, like sin, are generally dangerous. But there are potholes leaning on the above word of truth that do not endanger life, at least when they show up. They don't kill, steal, or destroy if we pay often onto their voices and address them. They are, if I may say so, part of the natural life of a man that alerts him to certain needs of the natural body.

Not only that, but they can equally play out in our spiritual lives, for there is always an equivalent of every natural phenomenon on the spiritual or supernatural plane.

Hunger:

Hunger is the voice of needs. It could be a need for food or drink (the latter is called thirst), a need for rest, help, companionship, sex, comfort, support, healing, deliverance, etc.

God put hunger in man as an alarm to notice that there is a need in his life. The absence or inadequacy of such a need could pose a danger if not addressed in me or adequately. This need increases as man grows and grapples with the affairs of life in this world. Hunger, for instance, is a natural and, to some extent, a supernatural alarm for bodily or spiritual needs, depending on the nature and source of the need.

A hunger for food or drink, for instance, requires that the man eat natural food and drink water, as that need is playing out in the natural body.

In that state of need, man feels a bit weak and dehydrated because the body has exhausted the nutrients and vitamins needed to support an active, healthy, and lively life due to work and the usage of stored energy from food and drink.

He needs to replenish, or else he continues on the downward trend of weakness and dehydration. If le unaddressed, this natural good pothole can turn harmful and endanger the life of the one it plagues, becoming a bad pothole. For this reason, every natural hunger should be addressed to ensure that life continues on a safe and healthy trajectory without breaking down, at least by reason of absence or non-response to those needs.

A deliberate disengagement, temporarily or permanently, from active work and a state of inactivity should be used to address a hunger or need for rest. This may include taking a break or leave of absence from work to replenish the exhausted energy due to use. However, experts posit that rest goes beyond bodily disengagement from active work. If the mind is not at rest, the bodily rest might not benefit much.

“Rest is in the mind," they contend. Sleep could be a good recipe for rest if it is wholesome. But not substance-induced sleep, which can give temporary rest but add to the burden of restlessness later and turn the situation into a bad pothole.

As for the hunger for companionship, make good friends-in the family, place of residence, place of worship, work, and business-with human beings like us. We should learn to relate to others within the bounds of good taste and righteousness without violating their privacy or dignity.

This caution applies to every good pothole, that is, do it within the bounds of good taste. For instance, overeating, wrong eating in terms of type, me, and frequency, or drinking can challenge the body and overwhelm the organs engaged in processing the foods for good absorption and body use. So also, a hunger for anything. Moderation, prudence, and reasonableness are keys to wisdom in satisfying the hunger for those needs.

God, Himself observed from creation that it is not good for man to be alone. The only thing God observed as not good, (not that He created loneliness), but to the degree that Adam male could not see someone like him to relate with, God says, it was not good. The danger in that was God, seeing that intimacy between man and animal could result in unwanted desires in relationships. #Pothole.

He then created a helpmate, the Adam female to address the issue immediately.

You see, God saw a need and addressed it immediately, not allowing the pothole to fester. We should imitate and emulate God, in our attitude to potholes, especially as we are created in His image after His likeness.

Kind begets kind.

When we observe signs of potholes, fix it and don't allow it to fester and degenerate to a bad pothole to become sin unto death.

If your hunger for companionship is for the opposite sex, then go and marry with wise counsel if you can no longer hold body.

"DON'T BURN WITH SEXUAL PASSION"

In which case your behaviour towards the opposite sex, both in utterances and attitude, are not within good taste and adjudged inappropriate. Of course there are consequences for such inappropriate behaviours both before God and before man.

In these ways are all natural hungers, diagnosed, a ended to and resolved for healthy living and interactive relationships.

God Himself observed from creation that it is not good for man to be alone. The only thing God observed as not good was loneliness (not that He created it), but to the degree that Adam could not see someone like him-of the same nature-to relate with, God says, it was not good.

God saw that man being alone could result in intimacy between man and animals. This is dangerous, as it could result in unwanted desires in relationships. Pothole!

He then created a helpmate, the Adam female, to address the issue immediately.

You see, God saw a need and addressed it immediately, not allowing the pothole to fester. We should imitate and emulate God in our attitude toward potholes, especially as we are created in His image and after His likeness. Kind begets kind.
When we observe signs of potholes, we fix them and don't allow them to fester and degenerate into bad potholes that become sins unto death.

On the sacred plane, our Lord Jesus says this: "God blesses those who hunger and thirst for justice, for they will be satisfied." Mathew 5:6 NLT

Jesus metaphorically used hunger and thirst here as an allegory for a desire to see justice served in a world of injustices draining the spiritual energy of people. The word rendered justice here is 'righteousness' in the King James Authorized Version of the Bible.

Righteousness is the demand of God for sinful men to repent of their sins by confessing Jesus Christ, His Son, as their Lord and Saviour, to believe and live right after obtaining forgiveness for their sins through His blood. In this sense, the hunger to see men submit to the God of all creation, to believe, do, and live right, is one that is here presented as a good pothole, a desire that God promises to recognize, bless, and satisfy.

What if this promised desire is not even expressed by men, thus rejecting the offer of God to honour, bless, and satisfy such hungers and thirsts for righteousness? It then becomes a bad and dangerous pothole, one that God has promised to visit with a wrath in His judgment because men refused to express this hunger, choosing instead to embrace the gaping and dangerous pothole of sin that can swallow them to death.

On the contemporary level, following from the examples of both the natural and supernatural potholes of hunger, a hunger to see some ills in society corrected, the needs of people met, justice served, or certain things done in certain ways for the best result, etc., is a pointer to the talents or gifts innate in a man that should be explored deeper.

Failure, or the absence of this good hunger for societal good, would be a waste of talents and gifts to the detriment of the person in particular and the society at large.

Example: Can you imagine the outcome if Mordecai and Queen Esther in the book of Esther had not risen to work together in defence of the Jews, who were facing the risk of annihilation and genocide by one man called Haman?

Can you imagine if Jesus did not confront Saul, turn him to the Apostle Paul, and draft him into ministry? Before the encounter, Apostle Paul was passionate about the tradition of his fathers to enforce all the tenets of the Jewish tradition and religion.

God saw his zeal and dexterity and decided to employ him to push the frontiers of salvation amongst the Gentile nations in particular, by someone with such a heart of compassion and the critical heart of the fanatical Jews.

People like Michael Jordan, Michael Angelo, the Abraham Lincolns of this world, Barack Obama, Nelson Mandela, The Great Pelle of Brazil, Dr. Nnamdi Azikiwe, Sir Ahmadu Bello, Chief Obafemi Awolowo, not forgetting Mother Theresa, and a host of others, etc., who distinguished themselves in their various callings in politics, ministry, sports, and entertainment, all had a hunger to make a difference and leave a footprint in the sands of history, a legacy that is speaking today.

QUESTIONS:

1. What needs have you noticed in yourself, your family, your place of worship, your residence, your neighbourhood, the nation, and society at large? Are you having an inner witness that you can do something about?
2. What are you passionate about?
3. What upsets you easily?
4. Have you engaged in any act of volunteerism before to solve a problem?
5. Do you have the desire to help anyone in a dire situation?

CHAPTER 3

DIAGNOSING A BAD POTHOLE

1. Then said he unto the disciples, it is impossible but that offences will come: but woe unto him, through whom they come! 2. It were better for him that a millstone was hanged about his neck, and he cast into the sea, than that he should offend one of these little ones. — (Luk 17:1-2, KJV)

Let's paraphrase and unpack the wisdom Jesus packed into the above truth He shared with His disciples as a guiderail.

1. Don't expect an offence or sin-free world.
2. As long as the earth remains, sin and its consequences will not cease.
3. However, those who either commit these sins or offences or cause others to sin shall pay a price for their roles in such a debacle of sins that is comparable to self-destruct.

Benchmarking this revelation with our conventional pothole, this would mean:

1. The construction company, whose unskilled staff did a bad and unprofessional job, probably by not properly diagnosing the topography of the area so as to determine the depth of excavation needed;
2. The company, after properly diagnosing and excavating the appropriate depth of soil, failed to use the appropriate materials to fortify the area to be water-resistant, such that a pothole was inevitable.
3. The government's supervisory agents, whether intentionally or unintentionally, neglected to address the company's poor performance and instead turned a blind eye.

Consequently, they have all positioned themselves on the path to self-destruction, as evident from the consequences outlined in the diagnostic interpretation of the scripture above.

On the other side of the equation, the party or agent of government whose duty it is to fix the bad pothole but fails to do so even when their attention has been drawn to it and possibly has misappropriated the budget allotted to it has committed a grave offence deserving no less punishment than the former if found guilty.

There are consequences not only because of possible official sanctions that could be invoked for inaction but also because of what I will call unintended consequences.

The consequences could range from loss of job to termination of contract, revocation of licence, prosecution, etc.

Let me explain the unintended consequences.

There is an adage that says those that live in a glass house should not throw stones, or, as in my local parable, -Throw not a stone in a crowded market, as the victim could be one of your relatives, especially your mother.

I watched a local film about a man who was a member of a fake drug cartel in their country. He made a lot of money from the illicit trade that he was well known for in the city.

The snag was that the wife did not know that the business the husband was into was the importation of fake drugs that were certainly killing people in great numbers.

There came a time when the man travelled out of the country on a business trip, plus a short holiday thereafter. He did not know that the wife was three months pregnant.

While away on the trip, the wife's pregnancy fever started and became very serious. Thinking that it was just some bouts of malaria fever, she sent their house help to go to the nearby chemist to fetch her a malaria drug over the counter. When the house help asked which one, she said anyone. Off, the house help went and, in me, returned with a certain stuff displayed as malaria drugs. She hurriedly took it, hoping that the fever and headache would subside in a matter of minutes or at most an hour's me.

After about 30 minutes, no change was in sight. In fact, the situation became bad and took a turn for the worse down the line.

To cut a long story short, it became an emergency case, and the husband, who was in constant touch with home and monitoring the situation, had to put a call across to a close friend to go check her up. The friend could not believe what he saw, as the woman was vomiting blood and stooling ceaselessly. An emergency vehicle was arranged to take her to the hospital. Unfortunately, she could not make it back home alive. The baby and the woman were lost.

The husband cut his trip short and dashed back home, only to see the corpse of his wife, with, of course, the dead three-month-old child still inside her.

His fear that his wife must have been a victim of his wicked act in illicit fake drug importation was founded, as his investigation revealed. Even his friend knew that was the case.

That film may have been fiction, drawing attention to how fake drugs were killing people, including relatives of the perpetrators, by whatever yardstick you define relatives.

In that metaphorical film of allegories lies the truth of what Jesus was telling the disciples: Woe to him, by whom offence comes.

As already stated, it is impossible to have a pothole-free world, both in absolute and figurative terms. As long as this earth remains, it is impossible to have a world free of offences, fraud, worry, fraud, lies, embezzlement, wrath, bitterness, stealing, sexual immorality, etc.

Bad potholes, as we choose to call them at this stage, start out small and appear malignant when left unattended.

Experts will tell you that before a road pothole appears, you will observe unusual features in the area. They could be in the form of water logs or cracks, indicating that the area is not properly fixed.

At this point, correctional action should be taken immediately after investigating the cause of the unusual features. Such an investigation must trace the cause to the root to solve and resolve it permanently.

Accordingly, a headache could be resolved by taking a painkiller. But where such a headache refuses to go away after taking the painkiller or keeps recurring, then the pain is a sign of a bigger pothole that should be traced and resolved before it becomes malignant, which is a bad and dangerous pothole that endangers life.

Generally, some potholes we classify as bad could be good at the first level of diagnosis, but may become malignant if not resolved in me.

For example, debt could be good if the proceeds of such debt are properly utilised to create assets that would yield good income. This entails investing the loan in projects or outlets that would yield returns within a defined me. To be roundly good, the returns should be such that they will take care of both the principal and interest repayments over a defined period of me.

Where this is not feasible or where debts are created to increase one's liabilities, having been used in consumables and consumption, it becomes a bad pothole that can wreck the happiness and financial growth of the victim.

Allowing debts to fester and failing in repayment programs is a dangerous pothole, and this could be due to poor diagnosis, execution, and/or manipulations, especially in the public sector.

This is true whether at the personal, group, corporate, or national levels.

Another pothole that could start out good and end up bad and dangerous, thus endangering life, is anger. Don't take my word for it. God says so:

Ephesians 4:26. Be ye angry, and sin not: let not the sun go down upon your wrath:

Here is Wikipedia online dictionary definition of anger

Strong feeling of displeasure, hostility or antagonism towards someone or something, usually combined with an urge to harm, often stemming from perceived provocation, hurt, or threat.

You can see that this definition agrees with what God says about anger. We can divide the phenomenon of anger into two parts.

The first part of anger is when this emotion rises in the mind and is up and running until this strong feeling of displeasure, hostility, or antagonism is accompanied by an urge to harm. In this first part, the anger could be good because it's a natural instinct to communicate our disapproval of something. Whether our displeasure or disapproval is right, justified, or not is a matter of opinion and depends on the person making the judgment.

Anger at this stage can also be a barometer to show us what we are gifted to do better than we are currently doing.

The second part is when this feeling of displeasure and/or disapproval goes into the urge to harm the person or the thing that caused, stokes, or drives the anger. This is the bad pothole part, a rage that should be avoided.

God warns us against such rage and says that anyone who goes to this level is likely to commit a heinous crime of sin with serious consequences. At this point, God says it is rage or wrath that can hang the disobedient who fails to take control of his emotions and allows them to get the better of him or her.

Danger looms; back off and get out now! An inner voice warns. Here is why.

19. Wherefore, my beloved brethren, let every man be swift to hear, slow to speak, slow to wrath:

20. For the wrath of man worketh not the righteousness of God. (Jam 1:19-20, KJV) "You can't be right with God, if you are a man of wrath" God says.

Anger that goes out of control and enters into wrath to harm and possibly carries out the harm cannot be justified in the sight of God or man.

If we accept that we are created in the image and likeness of God, then we should be able to exercise control over our emotions through the power of the Holy Spirit that indwells us. Don't judge or decide for God when anger is your gavel. It doesn't fit.

According to the above scripture, one way to control anger is to be slow to speak. There is strength in quietness-not that we should accommodate evil, but wisdom is profitable to direct. The best possible approach to not allowing anger to turn into violence is to speak less and leave the scene or stage of the rage. Speaking often and responding to every issue that comes your way can pit you against others and arouse anger.

"Sin is not lacking in the multitude of words..." Prov. 10:19, KJV, the scripture says.

Watch!

Should not the multitude of words be answered? and should a man full of talk be justified?
Job 11:2

In the multitude of words there wanteth not sin: but he that refraineth his lips is wise. Proverbs 10:19, KJV

In the above text, Job asked a question and with the benefit of hindsight, we know how his case turned out. Then Solomon answers in Pro. 10:19 and James caps it up in the text earlier quoted. One man who failed this test woefully, indeed the first, and paid a price was Cain. He was the first son of Adam, who, out of envy and anger, killed his brother Abel and robbed himself of the blessings of God.

The second was that great prophet of God, who was even described as the meekest man under heaven apart from Jesus, who lost his destiny under heaven (not the kingdom of God)-Moses.

We read about this story in Numbers 20:1–13. Though it is not specifically mentioned that Moses was angry, his disobedient action against the command of God was reprehensible, hence he was rebuked and sanctioned immediately by God. Some interpret his words as calling the children God had chosen 'rebels' and saw himself as God that supplies the water by saying 'us'. His action of striking the rock instead of speaking was prideful and needed to be checked. God did, and swiftly too.

Pride and anger are closely related. Sometimes anger is a medium to express pride, especially if one is not having his way and refuses to see things other people's way.

Do you have one?

CHAPTER 4

POTHOLES LOCALIZED, DOMESTICATED AND DOMICILED

Genesis 6:5-6, KJV

5. And GOD saw that the wickedness of man *was* great in the earth, and *that* every imagination of the thoughts of his heart *was* only evil continually.

6. And it repented the LORD that he had made man on the earth, and it grieved him at his heart.

As could be seen from the above text, the sin of man, here described as wickedness, became great in the earth, grew in heaps and bands, and went forward so much that it was now the lifestyle of man continually.

He became used to wickedness, domesticated and domiciled it in his domain, and localized it in his relationships.

God saw a big and dangerous pothole of hell swallowing man and expressed regret that He made him. Something had to be done about it.

How did we get here?

It could be said in modern times.
God Almighty decided to do something about the pothole of wickedness.

7. And the LORD said, I will destroy man whom I have created from the face of the earth; both man, and beast, and the creeping thing, and the fowls of the air; for it repenteth me that I have made them.
8. But Noah found grace in the eyes of the LORD. (Genesis 6:7-8, KJV)

The pothole of wickedness was 'closed' or checked by Almighty God through the destruction of the first world with the flood that wiped away everything on the surface of the earth, including man and beasts, except a family of eight people, the family of Noah, that found grace in the sight of God. (More on this later.)

Without question, for over 150 years, Noah preached repentance from violence and wickedness to the people of the first world, but no one heeded him, including possibly the members of his family. Not even when God asked Noah to start preparing the ark in which those that would be saved from the flood would be accommodated changed the minds of people.

Thousands of years after that flood, the potholes of wickedness and violence have taken hold of many lives in diverse ways around the world. This is notwithstanding the fact that God, who destroyed that first world, has provided a very soul-friendly way of escape from wickedness and violence.

Here are some dangerous potholes that we can diagnose in different places, both in low and high places.

INDIVIDUALS

- Lying
- Deceits and manipulations
- Covetousness
- Pride
- Blasphemy
- Boasting
- Disobedience
- Unthankfulness

- Unholiness
- Truce breaking
- False accusation
- Incontinent
- Fierceness
- Dismiss those that are good.
- Treacherousness
- Headiness
- High-mindedness
- Love of pleasure more than love of God.
- Having a form of godliness and denying the power thereof
- Ever learning, but never able to come to the knowledge of the truth.

FAMILIES, GROUPS & COMMUNITIES

- Hatred towards one another
- Bitterness against one another
- Strife and Hurt
- Rivalry
- Manipulations and deceit.
- Maneuvering to get ahead at the expense of others.

- Blind sightedness
- Infidelity
- Unfair deals and fraud
- Conflict of interests
- Poor delivery and outright failed promises on deals made.
- Faking, frauds and falsification of records.
- Indiscipline in varied degrees.

MARRIAGES AND RELATIONSHIPS GENERALLY

- Fear
- Infidelity
- Suspicion
- Breaches, crossing boundaries
- Unfaithfulness
- High handedness
- Ingratitude
- Impatience
- Indecision
- Indiscretion
- Insincerity
- Incontinence
- Condescending

- Complacency
- Complexity
- Lukewarmness
- Sickness
- Jealousy
- Ungodliness

PLACES OF LEARNING AND WORSHIP.

- Indiscipline
- Compromises on standards.
- Manipulations
- Discriminations
- Sexual immorality in various forms
- Malpractices and Cheating
- Bullying and violence
- Unfaithfulness
- Disobedience
- Child abuse
- Ingratitude.
- Witchcraft
- Drug abuse
- Stealing

- Revelling
- False teaching
- Rebellion
- Lying
- Prayerlessness
- Social malaise
- Restiveness
- Absence or lack of fear of God.

GOVERNMENT & CORPORATE BODIES

- Lack of vision
- Bribery and corruption
- Tribalism, nepotism, racism & nazism
- Favoritism
- Unprofessionalism or unskilled workforce.
- Impunity
- Electoral fraud
- Infidelity
- Tardiness and sloppiness
- Looting and outright fraud at all levels
- Incompetence, round pegs in square holes
- Aging and aged workforce.

- Lack of vision and will to execute, even if there is one.

The list in each heading is by no means exhaustive. Many more could be added. But it's not about the comprehensiveness of the list or otherwise. It is about the spirit behind them. The foul, unclean, demonic spirit of Satan and the fallen angels blinds the eyes of men, causing them to behave like beasts and ping them against their creator. It started in the garden, and the modus operandi has not changed. Deception, manipulation, manoeuvring, and lying to manifest ahead of others are all part of the spirit drive. It steals, kills, and ultimately destroys.

Resisting him with the truth is the only way out. The truth is that the potholes in individuals also play out in families, marriages, groups, communities, places of worship, schools, neighbourhoods where they live, and, anywhere they belong, relate to, and/or work. People make up groups, families, organizations, nations, etc.

An entity is only as good as the people that make it up. If the rules of engagement in those places do not check them, the potholed characters manifest, grow, and become malignant.

Accordingly, the character of a family, group, body, or government is the dominant character of the individuals that make up that community, body, and/or nation.

It is the sum total, or part thereof, of the individual members of the family, group, community, organization, and/or nation, such that it becomes their identity.

You can mention a family, and what shows up is stealing, prostitution, lying or telling the truth, helping, etc. This was probably the basis on which the law operated. If one steals, all steal, and vice versa.

I was once led to see how a person who had not even visited a country could have a good idea of what the people of the land are like. Just watch what happens at the entry points of that nation-the airports, train stations, seaports, or land borders.

Second, pick one or two local tabloids, and you will be greeted with a good sense of the character, morals, and dispositions of the people of the land, even before you encounter them one-on-one.

When you walk into any office, the character of the occupants is manifested in what you see on their tables and all around them.

Then listen to them.

To test the marital temperature of a married couple, just listen to them within minutes of engagement, and your eyes and ears will be filled with what is playing out in the marriage.

Scripture says, Your sin will find you out. It is impossible to hide our sins from God. We may try to hide it from men, but it won't be for too long-not from men and, of course, from yourself.

CHAPTER 5

THE DYNAMICS OF SIN OF UNRIGHTEOUSNESS AND OBEDIENCE IN RIGHTEOUSNESS (1)

---

33. Wisdom is enshrined in an understanding heart; wisdom is not found among fools. 34.
Godliness makes a nation great, but sin is a disgrace to any people.
35. A king rejoices in wise servants but is angry with those who disgrace him. Proverbs 14:33-35 NLT

The Hebrew word for 'nation' is 'gôy', pronounced 'go'-ee.

Meaning "people". A group of people of the same identity, under the same language, government, and territory (living together)
In Greek, the word is 'ĕthnõs', meaning 'a company or multitude of people of the same nature or genius. Ethnicity is, in English, a race or tribe of the same or accustomed to the same habit.

When used in the singular, it usually refers to the Jewish nation (example: Luke 7:5; 33:2; John 11:48), but if used in the plural (nations), it refers to any other nation other than the Jews. See Ma. 4:5; Rom. 3:29.

Source: Strong's Exhaustive Concordance of the Bible.

In my little way, with insight from the Word of God, and based on the above and in the context of this divine project, a nation is a community of people professing and manifesting common characteristics, which could be good or bad, godly or satanic, obedient or disobedient, right or wrong, true or false.

Members of this community may or may not be of the same colour, live in the same earthly location, be under the same earthly government, jurisdiction, or jurisprudence, and have the same culture and manners. Anywhere they are found, they are united in faith and belief.

A BIT OF HISTORY FOR PERSPECTIVE

At creation, God created Adam and Eve, who became husband and wife, to point out the truth that life is essentially about relationships.

Talking about relationships, Adam and Eve were created in the image of God, after His likeness. This means that they possessed defined qualities of God in capacity (inside light) and capability (outside abilities).

When you see them in this context and description, and how they speak, what they do, and where they are found, they are every inch of the way like God.

The exclamation would be, "Wow! No wonder," meaning exactly what Satan said concerning Job and what the Pharisees said in Acts 4, concerning the disciples whom they called IDIOTS.

Acts 4:13-The members of the council were amazed when they saw the boldness of Peter and John, for they could see that they were ordinary men with no special training in the Scriptures. They also recognized them as men who had been with Jesus.
You see the WOW there?

Accordingly, nationhood started at creation, when the first family was, in many ways, comparable to their creator, God Almighty.

There was only one location: the Garden of Eden, east of which man was located and housed. There was one language, truth, and one occupation-keeping and dressing the garden. They ate, interacted, and fellowshipped under one social and cultural umbrella.

However, God, who knows the end from the beginning, also gave an indication that there are exceptions.

1. Putting man in the east of the Garden of Eden, where He planted four rivers and fruit bearing trees, and commanding them to keep and dress it (watch over it), meant that man was restricted to that corner and was not to concern himself with anything outside the garden. He was to ensure that there was no intruder into the living area in the east because it was holy.

God used to meet them there at the cool of every evening (fellowship), hence it was sacred. The Garden was therefore like the Jewish nation that God chose as His firstborn, a chosen generation, a holy people, while the areas outside the garden could be regarded as the nations, the gentiles.

2. Even within the garden, there was an exception, as God said:

15. The LORD God placed the man in the Garden of Eden to tend and watch over it.
16. But the LORD God warned him, “You may freely eat the fruit of every tree in the garden
17. Except the tree of the knowledge of good and evil. If you eat its fruit, you are sure to die. Gen. 2:15-17.

These exceptions therefore became visible potholes that man must not violate or disobey if he is to avoid the consequence, which is death.

VIOLENCE IN VIOLATION OF ORDER

4. And the serpent said unto the woman, Ye shall not surely die:
5. For God doth know that in the day ye eat thereof, then your eyes shall be opened, and ye shall be as gods, knowing good and evil.
6. And when the woman saw that the tree was good for food, and that it was pleasant to the eyes, and a tree to be desired to make one wise, she took of the fruit thereof, and did eat, and gave also unto her husband with her; and he did eat. (Gen 3:4-6, KJV)

1. First, the serpent entered the living area. That's violation number one.

Who is the serpent?

It was the male Adam who named all the animals. He called him Serpent, the most subtle of all the beasts. To confirm the deceptive nature of this cattle, which agreed to be the transporter of the cursed and cast down Lucifer from heaven, he decided to engage the female Adam, Eve, who probably had little or no knowledge of him.

He attacked her with the very truth God told them, cast doubt in her mind, and the deed was done.

2. God says they would die: In the day that they eat it, they shall surely die.
3. The serpent told Eve that they would surely not die, adding that God knew that if they did, their eyes would open as gods, knowing good and evil.

The devil literally accused God of being a deceiver, whereas he is the deceiver. That's the common characteristic of fraudsters: deception and accusation at the same me.

4. The woman agreed to hear the voice of a stranger and fully subscribed to investing all her life in the invisible empire of the devil.
5. She didn't die alone; she convinced her husband to commit suicide with her.

We know the rest of the story.
When they ate the fruit of knowledge of good and bad, it appeared as though all was going well until this happened:

7. And the eyes of them both were opened, and they knew that they were naked; and they sewed fig leaves together, and made themselves aprons.

8. And they heard the voice of the LORD God walking in the garden in the cool of the day: and Adam and his wife hid themselves from the presence of the LORD God amongst the trees of the garden. (Gen 3:7-8, KJV)

You see, when they ate the forbidden fruit, their colour, physique, and height remained intact.

However, the glory of God, which had been their light inside and garment outside, departed, and an apron of shame in their nakedness opened up.

The first place disobedience does damage is on the inside. The spirit died, and so they died spiritually that same day, and the vista of shame opened.

The evidence is the shame they had not known or experienced before, now activated and operative.

Secondly, they wanted to skip daily fellowship with God in the cool of the evening of that day.

The voice of God became a terror in their sinful flesh, which could not stand the holy voice of God.

"How do you feel or respond to the message of the gospel hing and hammering on something on the inside?"

When was the last me you checked on that brother or sister who has not come to church or a meeting or picked up his or her phone in a long while?

He or she might be baling with something. A visit is indicated.

What of a co-worker who used to be very prompt and active at work, and all of a sudden he or she started skipping work, being very lethargic, and even making a lot of blunders on the work he or she used to be very good at?

How about that regular customer you have not seen in a long while?

The truth is that changes in attitude, choice of words, or places where one is found are indications of life issues pushing one in the right or wrong direction. Either way, we should be our brother's keepers when the indications point to a departure from good.

CHAPTER 6

THE DYNAMICS OF SIN OF UNRIGHTEOUSNESS AND OBEDIENCE IN RIGHTEOUSNESS (2)

As already indicated, when Adam and Eve conspired with the devil to sin against God, it seemed inconsequential to them (a negligible pothole) until the one who sees the end from the beginning arrived at the scene, and this happened:

9. And the Lord God called unto Adam, and said unto him, Where art thou?
10. And he said, I heard thy voice in the garden, and I was afraid, because I was naked; and I hid myself.
11. And he said, Who told thee that thou wast naked? Hast thou eaten of the tree, whereof I commanded thee that thou shouldest not eat?
12. And the man said, The woman whom thou gavest to be with me, she gave me of the tree, and I did eat.
13. And the Lord God said unto the woman, What is this that thou hast done? And the woman said, The serpent beguiled me, and I did eat." (Gen 3:9-13, KJVA)

Here is, in passing, what we can learn from the above:

1. Sin truncates fellowship and terrifies the sinner.
2. First, they knew they were naked and open to more attacks because fellowship with God is broken. - vulnerable

3. To nakedness, fear is added.
4. Sin pushes us to hide from God. This is the simple reason why many do not want to come to the light: because their deeds are evil. (John 3:18)
5. Though sin breaks fellowship, in truth, it does not separate us from the love of God. Truly and really, God loves the sinner but hates sin with perfect hatred. We can be restored because God would never leave us or forsake His inheritance for the devil. He wants the sinner to repent and be restored. (CLOSE THE POTHOLE TO AVOID CRASHING FURTHER AND DEEPER.)
6. Sin has consequences and must be judged.

14. And the LORD God said unto the serpent, Because thou hast done this, thou art cursed above all cattle, and above every beast of the field; upon thy belly shalt thou go, and dust shalt thou eat all the days of thy life:

15. And I will put enmity between thee and the woman, and between thy seed and her seed; it shall bruise thy head, and thou shalt bruise his heel. (Gen 3:14-15, KJV)

7. Above was the judgment God passed on sin and the ring leader, the Serpent.

Have you seen the movement of the serpent before? Curly, complicated, and twisted. That's one of the characteristics of fraudsters. Never straight in speech, movement, character, relationships, etc.

Did you see that God did not ask the serpent any questions? I am not even sure he was there when the trial was conducted and judgment passed.

Have nothing to do with the unfruitful work of darkness; instead, rebuke them. Adam and Eve did not escape sanctions for their roles in that violation of the sacred command of God. (Check it up.)

In addition, Adam and Eve were evicted from the Garden.

22. And the LORD God said, Behold, the man is become as one of us, to know good and evil: and now, lest he put forth his hand, and take also of the tree of life, and eat, and live forever: 23. Therefore the LORD God sent him forth from the Garden of Eden, to till the ground from whence he was taken.

24. So he drove out the man; and he placed at the east of the garden of Eden Cherubims, and a flaming sword which turned every way, to keep the way of the tree of life." (Gen 3:2224, KJV)

With the above, the immediate judgment of sin, with a clear indication of the consequences, was completed, but not without God demonstrating His heart of mercy and love.

Unto Adam also and to his wife did the LORD God make coats of skins, and clothed them. (Gen 3:21, KJV)

You can see clearly from the above both the immediate and unintended consequences of the potholes we alluded to earlier, now from a biblical perspective.

Do you think Adam and Eve would have dared to disobey God if they knew their action, which lasted but for a moment, would cost them this much?

It took God, not the devil, who lied to the Adams about and against God, to notice sin as that which is contrary to his word, judge sin, punish the sinners with a clear indication that it was a suspended sentence (more would be served, see v. 15), and of course temporarily give a holding aid to stop the damage.

In summary, everything seemed inconsequential until further down the line, when more fruit of sin appeared, taking it to another level because the pothole was widening. This happened:

3. And in process of me it came to pass, that Cain brought of the fruit of the ground an offering unto the LORD. 4. And Abel, he also brought of the firstlings of his flock and of the fat thereof. And the LORD had respect unto Abel and to his offering:

5. But unto Cain and to his offering he had not respect. And Cain was very wroth, and his countenance fell.

6. And the LORD said unto Cain, Why art thou wroth? and why is thy countenance fallen?

7. If thou doest well, shalt thou not be accepted? and if thou doest not well, sin lieth at the door. And unto thee shall be his desire, and thou shalt rule over him.

8. And Cain talked with Abel his brother: and it came to pass, when they were in the field, that Cain rose up against Abel his brother, and slew him. (Gen 4:3-8, KJV)

Cain and Abel were the first two offspring of Adam and Eve. In fact, some believe they were twins, but even if they were, the general view is that Cain is the elder.

Out of envy and anger, Cain slew and killed his brother Abel, despite God's warning.

For the first me, God called the wrong done to Him and our fellow human's sin.

It was grivious and heinous to ignore it and address it for what it is. Call it out in order to situate the problem and apply the appropriate response in sanction and prevention.

This was the first culpable homicide in the flesh. The first was the death of the spirit of the Adams, leaving them with the flesh.

Since it was the tree of the knowledge of good and bad that they ate, and based on the principle of "kind begets kind", it was not surprising that they brought forth good and bad children. Abel was good, and, of course, Cain was bad, by reason of the quality of their sacrifices to God.

It is not clear why God did not have respect for the offering of Cain, but scholars believe that it was not unconnected to the bloodless nature of his sacrifice. Those children must have been taught what an acceptable sacrifice to God should be, but Cain chose to go against it, bearing that bad seed, which revealed the state of his heart.

There is no remission of sin without the shedding of blood. Accordingly, by not offering a bloody sacrifice, Cain disputed and rejected the judgment of God, saying that sin had been committed against him and needed to be atoned for according to His command. He thus made God a liar, after the manner of the serpent who accused God in the garden. (1 john 1:10)

"You are servant to who you choose to obey"— Rom 6:16

Thus, anger, hate, envy, wrath, and now murder manifest as part of the fruit of sin. When God confronted Cain, he feigned ignorance and had the contrived spirit of boldness to ask God a question, the first recorded in the Bible.

And the LORD said unto Cain, Where is Abel thy brother? And he said, I know not: Am I my brother's keeper? (Gen 4:9, KJV)

Fraudsters usually manifest a deceptive character of boldness on the outside but weakness and terror on the inside.

Adam and Eve ran and hid themselves when they heard the voice of God after their crimes. Cain stood on slippery ground, faced God, and had the effrontery to ask God a question. Sinners become bolder and dig deeper the longer they stay in sin, excusing and defending it at their peril. —Potholes

Cain, like his parents, received a due reward for his sins, was banished from the presence of God, and was declared a persona non granta (fugive and vagabond, wanderer).

Sin renders the heart and mind confused, deserted, and fruitless in righteousness. All acts of unrighteousness are sin before God, but the sin of shedding blood is totally unacceptable to God and has grave consequences. God says He will require the blood of the offender.

Watch!

5. And surely your blood of your lives will I require; at the hand of every beast will I require it, and at the hand of man; at the hand of every man's brother will I require the life of man.

6. Whoso sheddeth man's blood, by man shall his blood be shed: for in the image of God made the man. (Gen 9:5-6, KJV)

Taking the life of another is the peak of unrighteousness, which God would judge harshly no matter what. But we know that sin began with the seemingly harmless lie the devil, or Satan, told the children of God in the Garden of Eden. It turned out that that sin of lies did not just harm Adam and Eve but cost them everything they had—wisdom, glory, power, relationship with God, free accommodation, provisions, protection, etc.—and opened them up to nakedness, fear, confusion, shame, accusation, suffering, hardship, lack, and even death, as it were.

"One without God is as good as a dead person."

God's love for them, however, remained unchanged as He put in place a temporary measure to stabilize their wounded spirit and cover their nakedness with the blood of an animal and her skin, respectively.

From that time of the temporary measure to the time sin entered the second generation through Cain, sin took a turn for the worst. The pothole kept widening and expanding in depth and spread.

What began as a small pothole dug a gully in the hearts of men, spreading like wildfire and burning down anything on its path like a hurricane across subsequent generations.

God was watching and taking His me to activate and actualize His promise in Gen. 3:15 to address the problem of sin.

This is because God already had a plan before the world was created, which man, in conspiracy with the devil, could delay at their peril but couldn't alter.

Merciful God even listened to Cain when he protested his sentence, and God put a curse on anyone that would kill Cain in the course of his wandering around in confusion as a fugitive and vagabond.

11. And now art thou cursed from the earth, which hath opened her mouth to receive thy brother's blood from thy hand;

12. When thou tillest the ground, it shall not henceforth yield unto thee her strength; a fugitive and a vagabond shalt thou be in the earth.

13. And Cain said unto the LORD, My punishment is greater than I can bear.

14. Behold, thou hast driven me out this day from the face of the earth; and from thy face shall I be hid;

and I shall be a fugitive and a vagabond in the earth; and it shall come to pass, that every one that findeth me shall slay me.

15. And the LORD said unto him, Therefore whosoever slayeth Cain, vengeance shall be taken on him sevenfold. And the LORD set a mark upon Cain, lest any finding him should kill him. (Gen 4:11-15, KJV)

The death of Abel, the good seed, meant that only evil was existing on earth through the bad seed, Cain, since Abel did not get the chance to procreate before his brutal death.

While God, was working on the reactivation of the good seed as truth, to counter the lies, which eventually happened through the birth of Seth to Adam & Eve, evil took off with its nave language, lies spread and dominated the earth with wickedness, but certainly running into the pothole of hell, unless light appears at the end of the tunnel. The resultant picture is addressed in our next chapter.

CHAPTER 7

THE REIGN OF EVIL ON EARTH THROUGH LIES - THE FATHER AND MOTHER OF POTHOLES

1. Then the people began to multiply on the earth, and daughters were born to them.
2. The sons of God saw the beautiful women and took any they wanted as their wives.
5. The LORD observed the extent of human wickedness on the earth, and he saw that everything they thought or imagined was consistently and totally evil.
6. So the LORD was sorry he had ever made them and put them on the earth. It broke his heart. Gen. 6:1-2, 5-6.

What you see above is a state of confusion and disorder on earth that lies produced and gave birth to.

Many believe that the sons of God under reference were the fallen angels, while others believe they are the offspring of the new good seed, Seth, who was already born.

The latter appears more like it since they are described as sons of God, meaning they possessed real human bodies and could sexually mix with irrational daughters of men, possibly from the bad seed side of Cain, who took off first.

The entry into the world of sin means there are two languages in the world: truth and lies. You are either telling the truth or lying.
Lie is the mother and father of all sins of wickedness and violence on earth. Every other pothole of wickedness in unrighteousness starts from this sin, as its brother, sister, uncle, aunt, cousin, niece, nephew, etc. Lying to oneself, to family and friends, to your wife, children, brothers and sisters, groups you belong to, the school you a end or a ended, the business you do, your clients, customers, and stakeholders; lying to your leader or leaders, to your citizens, colleagues, and neighbours, and lying to your doctor as to the true nature of your ailment or to your lawyer regarding the offence committed. Lying to governmental authorities concerning your actions, decisions, responsibilities, and true intentions. Likewise, lying to God, your creator, who knows all things, is everywhere at the same time, sees all things, and hears all things, even the unspoken words of the heart, who cannot be deceived or lied to.

This is why we made it number one on our lists of acts of unrighteousness across a broad spectrum of existential pothole threats.

The damage lies can do to people, families, groups, organizations, and nations is so devastating that what God saw grieved His heart.
He made a decision to destroy the whole world, sparing only one family, not necessarily because they were faultless, but because the integrity of the head of that family stood taller than any in that world, and the Lord of all the earth took a stand to reward him.

7. And the LORD said, "I will wipe this human race I have created from the face of the earth. Yes, and I will destroy every living thing—all the people, the large animals, the small animals that scurry along the ground, and even the birds of the sky. I am sorry I ever made them."
8. But Noah found favor with the LORD. Genesis 6:7-8 NLT

Do not be deceived; sin has consequences. If you think otherwise and feel it's cheap, just tell a lie, and the pothole will appear like a harmless dot, but its true cost, which is very expensive, especially if allowed to fester, will sooner or later take hold and become obvious to you, even in your pretence. It will wake you up from sleep, which does not cover it.

Sin is so expensive that, in the above biblical account under review, we are told for the first me that it is something that grieved the heart of Almighty God, given the malignant and dominant status it has attained over me. He was sorry that He made man and put him on earth.

This is Almighty God, expressing regret over His handiwork—me and you. Think about that. Would you like to lose your inheritance, spouse, child, job, brother or sister, parents, relatives, friends, money, investments, etc. to fraudsters (robbers, kidnappers, and hijackers)? Yet the biggest of them all is when death snatches a sinner who refuses to repent from sin. What transaction or relationship at any level—marriage, ministry, business, government, investment, tenancy, help, journey—have you been involved in, and now, looking back, you wish you never did?

On the other side of the coin, what lies have you told yourself, your parents, partners, employers, colleagues, clients, customers, members, worshippers, friends, families, etc. with respect to your true identity, qualifications, origin, products, and services offered and rendered? Transactions engaged in, playing smart, smiling home with blood proceeds in pecuniary and material gains that seemingly put you ahead that you now regret and wish you never did?

Does this afford you an opportunity to examine your ways and change them, or do you want to dig deeper?

Recall, that's where we started and what led to this project. An investment, or should I say, investment relationships, I entered into back in the days, when I was still working, to provide for myself today, when I retire and am not so much into active work and earning.

Fifteen (15) years later, they are still in limbo. Mortal men who were frequenting my office, persuading me with sweet tongues to invest in properties, shares, forex trading, etc., are now evasive and elusive. I am now the one frequenting their offices (for those that can be located), pleading that they honour and deliver on their promises. You spend money pursuing what ordinarily is supposed to be straightforward, leaving you no option but to believe that the whole thing was a scam from the beginning. #Potholes.

If you think I am alone on this, you'd better think again.

There are many with me on this ship, sailing to nowhere. This is not because we are that gullible, but because dubious men with immoral intentions and questionable characters surround us.

In my own case, one of them is even a known deacon in a very big Pentecostal church in our country. It was unknown to me that he not only had the Bible in one hand but also a satanic sword in the other to kill and maim.

God made a decision. You need to make a decision, too. What would your decision be? God Almighty does not issue an empty threat. He has the right and capacity to execute anything that suits him and the plans he envisioned when he set out to create the world. Now that the world He created has, by the choices of men, gone after lies, been defaced, and, by that, changed the face and trajectory of the world, man can only have and exercise this wicked choice to some extent. God, by choice, contrary to the choices of men, has had the last say to show the right way since the entry of sin, provided an alternative language to truth, and made choice an option.

Keep this in mind, for truth is irrevocable and irreversible.

IT IS GOD WHO HAS THE FINAL SAY AND THE FINAL WAY, NOT MAN.

To demonstrate the veracity of the above truth, which is in the status of law, this happened in judgment of sin and unrepentant sinners.

THE PREPARATION FOR THE JUDGMENT

11 Now God saw that the earth had become corrupt and was filled with violence.

12 God observed all this corruption in the world, for everyone on earth was corrupt.

13 So God said to Noah, "I have decided to destroy all living creatures, for they have filled the earth with violence. Yes, I will wipe them all out along with the earth!

14 "Build a large boat from cypress wood and waterproof it with tar, inside and out. Then construct decks and stalls throughout its interior.

15 Make the boat 450 feet long, 75 feet wide, and 45 feet high.

16 Leave an 18-inch opening below the roof all the way around the boat. Put the door on the side, and build

three decks inside the boat—lower, middle, and
upper.
19 "Bring a pair of every kind of animal—a male and a
female—into the boat with you to keep them alive
during the flood.
20 Pairs of every kind of bird, and every kind of animal,
and every kind of small animal that scurries along
the ground, will come to you to be kept alive.
21 And be sure to take on board enough food for your
family and for all the animals.
22 So Noah did everything exactly as God had
commanded him. Genesis 6:11-16, 19-22 NLT

THE OBEDIENCE TO THE COMMAND OF GOD

So Noah did everything exactly as God had commanded him. Genesis 6:22 NLT

Six is the number of man, and 22 is the number of manifestation and alignment. God created man on the sixth (6th) day in His image and likeness to manifest His glory.

Anything short of total obedience to the command of God, manifesting lies and wickedness (disobedience), attracts the judgment of God.

Noah did everything exactly as God instructed. Take note of that. He was a man who was not ashamed to stand alone with God, even when everybody was going in the opposite direction.

Can you stand alone when everybody is standing against the truth, or would you be a democrat and let the majority have the way?

What is the result?

CHAPTER 8

EXECUTION OF GOD'S RIGHTEOUS JUDGMENT ON SIN

7:1 When everything was ready, the Lord said to Noah, "Go into the boat with all your family, for among all the people of the earth, I can see that you alone are righteous.
7:3 Also take seven pairs of every kind of bird. There must be a male and a female in each pair to ensure that all life will survive on the earth after the flood.

7:4 Seven days from now I will make the rains pour
down on the earth. And it will rain for forty days and
forty nights, until I have wiped from the earth all the
living things I have created."
7:5 So Noah did everything as the Lord commanded
him.
7:11 When Noah was 600 years old, on the
seventeenth day of the second month, all the
underground waters erupted from the earth, and the
rain fell in mighty torrents from the sky.
7:12 The rain continued to fall for forty days and forty
nights.
7:13 That very day Noah had gone into the boat with
his wife and his sons—Shem, Ham, and Japheth—and
their wives.
7:14 With them in the boat were pairs of every kind of
animal—domestic and wild, large and small—along
with birds of every kind.
7:15 Two by two they came into the boat, representing
every living thing that breathes. 7:16 A male and a
female of each kind entered, just as God had
commanded Noah. Then the Lord closed the door
behind them. Genesis 7:1, 3-5, 11-16 NLT

1. Who is in charge here?

2. Where was the serpent that caused trouble for man in all of this?
3. Was the serpent among the beasts saved too? (Hold your answer to yourself.)
4. Did you notice that aquatic life was not affected because their natural habitat, water, was the instrument of judgment? Could this have anything to do with why fish became chief among foods, both in the Bible's days and even now?
5. Is it also a pointer to the fact that crossing boundaries is the precursor to sanctionable offences? [The serpent entered the living area where men were kept, having unfettered access to them, and the woman gave him the master's seat.]
6. What do you allow and entertain in your heart?

5. Have you seen where a fish is used in performing any sacrifice? (Send me pictures.) I love these two parts.

- God cares for the animals as much as He cares for men. They were both species created the same day, went down the same day, and were saved together in the same ark the same day, all by God Almighty, their creator and Saviour.

- It was God Almighty who performed the first "passenger help" service for mortal man. "Then the Lord closed the door behind them."

Play that in your mind and smile a smile of admiration unto our God, who loves and cares totally.

"May this compassionate, unfailing love of the Father encompass our hearts in a reciprocal gesture of appreciation."
Remember, the serpent, who was the transporter of the devil, opposed him, lied against him in the garden, and was there in that ark, albeit under judgment.

Yet, God Almighty personally closed the door of the ark; it was riding in to safety out of the world, and it was practically brought down in conspiracy with man, also on board.

Where was the devil all the while God gave instructions to Noah to prepare the ark, gather his family members, and determine the number of each species of beast on earth, preparatory to the destruction of the earth?

Why did he not attack or stop Noah, or even challenge the entire project of salvation, since God did not speak in secret concerning the impending doom? And even if he did, why did he not stop the salvation project, as it were?

It rained for forty (40) days on earth, and the resultant flood was on the face of the earth for 150 days, yet the serpent could not stop or reverse any aspect of those; instead, he became a victim of the judgment except for the lucky species duo that made it on board the ark.

What do we learn from all this?

1. God created the heavens and earth and the fullness thereof, not the devil, which is a creature.
2. God has all the power to decide the fate of the earth and all its inhabitants, including humans. A word from God can ruin the entire creation, and a word from God can also restore it, as He chooses.
1. All power belongs to God, and only He must be worshipped, as Jesus said during His temptation, where He mesmerized the devil. Every creature, including the arrogant Satan, must worship God.
2. The devil can neither stop God nor you if you are in alignment with God and obey His command. In this, Adam and Eve were found

wanting and were stopped, but Noah was in sync and received the highest honor from God.

- Jesus says that of all those given to Him, no one takes any from Him because His Father, who gave them to Him, is more powerful than any.
- The same applies to his own life, which he also says he had the power to lay down willingly and pick up again.
- The devil only has the power of lies and deception. Check out the content of the temptation of Our Lord, when the devil wanted to try what he did to Adam on Our Lord, the second Adam.

They were all suggestive. If the devil had the power of creation and enforcement, he would have converted the stone to bread and commanded Jesus to eat it, pushed him out of the pinnacle, or forced him to worship, or else XYZ would happen. He can't and couldn't because he can only suggest to you what to do, and when you do, which is usually a lie, you face the consequences alone, which he can't reverse or amend. Accordingly, the power the devil has is your power to say no, because it would offend God, and we don't receive instruction from the devil. He is an enemy of God who was cast out of heaven and is looking for many to take with him to the outer darkness. Don't let him. Stand with God.

- It's a big folly, for one to compromise on the word of God, blame everybody and anybody except himself like Adam and Eve. It can create a dangerous pothole like hell which can swallow everybody and anything like in the case of the judgment of the flood.
- If you wouldn't be proud of it and willing to share it with others and bequeath it to your children, don't do it, no matter how appealing and seemingly rewarding it appears. "All that glitters is not gold". There is a way that is pleasing to man, but it's a way that leads to destruction, as scripture says in Proverbs 14:12.
- The devil is as smart as you are willing to concede to him and allow him to get away with it. You are smarter, not all by yourself, but standing in agreement with God, even if it makes no sense, is all faith. "It is written," let it be by faith (agreement with God). Doing it for the sake of God in Christ Jesus.

5. God's word, not that of any man or creature, is the truth; every other word could be a fact but not the truth. There is only one truth that everybody should

embrace and speak: what God says; otherwise, you would be a victim of a lie you heard and told yourself.

When Jesus, who closed that door, tells us to love our enemies, He is not telling us to do what He has not done or would not do, as that would amount to hypocrisy.

By loving our enemies, we do not mean they have escaped justice. It means we have handed the judgment over to the righteous judge of all the earth, who sees and knows all things. He does it best, and when he does, there is no appeal anywhere. It is final.

Judas was one of the twelve. He chose to be a special messenger. He was the one who betrayed him, and Jesus knew that very well and allowed him to be in the fold. He even called him 'friend', in the midst of the betrayal.

Judas was to perform a different kind of special task in the life of our Lord—the one that, unknown to Judas, would have been a gateway to His glory. But he chose to crash at the gate and align with the enemies. It backfired on him, and he died before the death of our Lord on the cross.

The day for the final judgment is still ahead, even beyond the judgment of the flood, which did not stop the re-emergence of sin and the spreading of it, as we will see in the next chapters.

CHAPTER 9

A NEW WORLD EMERGED AFTER JUDGMENT EVENTS

1 But God remembered Noah and all the wild animals and livestock with him in the boat. He sent a wind to blow across the earth, and the floodwaters began to recede.
2 The underground waters stopped flowing, and the torrential rains from the sky were stopped.
3 So the floodwaters gradually receded from the earth. After 150 days,
4 exactly five months from the me the flood began, the boat came to rest on the mountains of Ararat.
5 Two and a half months later, as the waters continued to go down, other mountain peaks became visible. Genesis 8:1-5 NLT.

I decree and declare that every flood of judgment from the North, South, East, and West that is opened up against you and your household receives the wind of mercy of God, recedes, stops, and dries up, in the mighty name of Jesus Christ. Amen.

God would always remember, and he wants us to remember too. He remembered Noah and all the occupants of the ark, man and beast, not that He could forget, but that you should know that nothing escapes His sight. After all, He is omnipresent, everywhere at the same me, and all things lay bare before Him. Who reminded Him that something had gone amiss in the garden? All the questions He asked Adam and Eve were accountability motivated and driven. He is the God of justice and would want to give an offender the opportunity to state his side of the case against him in accordance with the principles of a fair trial and equity.

When He created the light, it was not because He wanted to see what He was doing; day and night are the same before Him. It was for you and me to see what He did, when, and how, so that we might replicate the ones He had given us the power to replicate.

Again, it took God's supernatural intervention to end the judgment, clean up the mess, and restore man to the earth that He had created and bequeathed to him in righteousness. God is neither late nor early in carrying out His plan. Whatever has happened, times and chance determined in eternity, happened to them.

Our prayers, fasting, vigil, anointing oil, etc., can never change, quicken, or delay the plans of God.
Here is why:

For we which have believed do enter into rest, as he said, As I have sworn in my wrath, if they shall enter into my rest: although the works were finished from the foundation of the world. Hebrews 4:3

You see, nothing is new. God had a plan before He set out to create the world, and one step at a time, He went about executing it. If you think that the sin of Adam and Eve caught God off guard, you'd better think again. Not possible.

Why do you think He called day and night one day, starting in the evening and not the morning? That shows that in every creature, including man, there is a dark part and a light part. So a day starts in the evening, followed by the morning, and not the other way around, as many believe. That's how activities are observed in the land of the Bible. The new day begins in the evening, not in the morning, as the nations observe. The first hour of prayer is 6 p.m.–9 p.m. until you come to the 8th, which is 3 p.m.–6 p.m. the following day to make a day.

3. And God said, Let there be light: and there was light.

4. And God saw the light, that it was good: and God divided the light from the darkness.
5. And God called the light Day, and the darkness he called Night. And the evening and the morning were the first day. (Gen 1:3-5, KJV)

Every man begins with darkness in this world, tainted with the sin of Adam.

A newborn baby comes with eyes closed and gradually opens the eyes over days or weeks as light continues to pour into the eyes. (There is a revelatory message there, exclusive to this project: I am not indifferent to what your science will tell you.)

As we are exposed to the message of the gospel, we are transformed from glory to glory, shining from brightness to brightness unto the perfect day.

But we all, with open face beholding as in a glass the glory of the Lord, are changed into the same image from glory to glory, even as by the Spirit of the Lord. (2 Cor 3:18, KJV)

Beholding here is in the present continuous tense. You continue to behold, and the more you behold, the more you are transformed. Get my book, Success

Mindset, for explosive devotional insights, knowledge, and wisdom.

But the path of the just is as the shining light, that shineth more and more unto the perfect day. Proverbs 4:18

3. All things were made by him; and without him was not anything made that was made.
4. In him was life; and the life was the light of men.
5. And the light shineth in darkness; and the darkness comprehended it not. John 1:3-5

God is light, and He would come at last as light in judgment to disperse every darkness in man and set up the kingdom of marvelous light that no darkness can comprehend. Even now, that kingdom stands sure on a rocky, not shaky, foundation, our Lord Jesus, and the gate of hell cannot prevail against it. The Church is the preview of the Kingdom of God on supernatural transit.

Under heaven, darkness can eclipse the light—the light of some mortal men who hold on to wickedness, refusing to come to the light (Deep).

Watch!

19. And this is the condemnation, that light is come into the world, and men loved darkness rather than light, because their deeds were evil.

20. For every one that doeth evil hateth the light, neither cometh to the light, lest his deeds should be reproved.

21. But he that doeth truth cometh to the light, that his deeds may be made manifest, that they are wrought in God. John 3:19-21

"God's remembrance is your remembrance of Him as Your good and faithful God, Who will never leave you nor forsake you"

15. Then God said to Noah,

16. "Leave the boat, all of you—you and your wife, and your sons and their wives.

17. Release all the animals—the birds, the livestock, and the small animals that scurry along the ground—so they can be fruitful and multiply throughout the earth."

18. 18. So Noah, his wife, and his sons and their wives le the boat.

19. And all of the large and small animals and birds came out of the boat, pair by pair. Genesis 8:15-19 NLT

Can you sense God in that scenario standing by the door of the ark yet again, opening it, and asking Noah and his family to disembark?
He further asked him to release the domestic and wild animals onboard the ark. Meaning that, as it was under Adam and Eve, the beasts of the field, the birds of the air, and the fish of the sea are all subject to man. Nothing has changed except the captain of the ship of the world, bodily, now Noah and his family.

God, who was there to close the door of the ark before the flood of judgment lied it, was there again to open the door, asking Noah and his family to disembark from the ark.

He watches over us, and He is the first and the last, Alpha and Omega (Rev 22:13). "We are safe in and with Him."

Here is the Messianic prophet Isaiah, who saw what we would be in Christ, the Ark of our Salvation:

16 Justice will rule in the wilderness and righteousness in the fertile field.

17 And this righteousness will bring peace. Yes, it will bring quietness and confidence forever.

18 My people will live in safety, quietly at home. They will be at rest.

19 Even if the forest should be destroyed and the city torn down,

20 the LORD will greatly bless his people. Wherever they plant seed, bountiful crops will spring up. Their cattle and donkeys will graze freely. Isaiah 32:16-20

This is the earthly Jerusalem that Isaiah saw. It is happening now in the midst of wickedness in the world that surrounds Israel, chosen of the Lord.

However, in Christ, it applies to the whole world when the covenants that preceded and followed Isaiah's prophecy are reviewed and connected. My book on Partake-to-Connect... is rich and insightful in this regard and more.

What do you think it would be like, in the heavenly Jerusalem, when wickedness would have been judged finally?

Awesome! Hope and hold on to God and His promises. He is faithful, as promised. "Do nothing; don't step out;

don't make the next move until you have heard the Lord's voice in your heart."

That way, and until then, enjoy the peace of His last command to you. Remain locked in Christ, our ark of salvation in redemption.

20 Then Noah built an altar to the LORD, and there
he sacrificed as burnt offerings the animals and
birds that had been approved for that purpose.
21 And the LORD was pleased with the aroma of
the sacrifice and said to himself, "I will never again
curse the ground because of the human race, even
though everything they think or imagine is bent
toward evil from childhood. I will never again
destroy all living things.
22 As long as the earth remains, there will be
planting and harvest, cold and heat, summer and
winter, day and night." Genesis 8:20-22 NLT

Whether it is in your waking up in the morning, the plan to marry and bring in your spouse, your first day in office, and indeed every day, the arrival of your new baby, the receipt of your pay check, the completion of the project, the arrival on that journey, your book launch, etc. Give God thanks in the sacrifice of praise and worship.

"IT IS GOOD TO GIVE THANKS" (Ps. 107:1).

Let him hear your voice thanking him from your heart. Don't ask him anything. Just a sweet-smelling and smiling savour in appreciation of what He has done for you. Here is how and why.

5 Trust in the LORD with all your heart; do not depend on your own understanding.
6 Seek his will in all you do, and he will show you which path to take.
7 Don't be impressed with your own wisdom. Instead, fear the LORD and turn away from evil.
8 Then you will have healing for your body and strength for your bones.
9 Honor the LORD with your wealth and with the best part of everything you produce.
10 Then he will fill your barns with grain, and your vats will overflow with good wine. Proverbs 3:5-10

After Noah's sacrifice, God re-establishes and reconfirms His covenant with man, as He did with Adam thus:

12 Then God said, "I am giving you a sign of my
covenant with you and with all living creatures, for all
generations to come.
13 I have placed my rainbow in the clouds. It is the sign
of my covenant with you and with all the earth.
14 When I send clouds over the earth, the rainbow will
appear in the clouds,
15 and I will remember my covenant with you and
with all living creatures. Never again will the
floodwaters destroy all life.
16 When I see the rainbow in the clouds, I will
remember the eternal covenant between God and
every living creature on earth."
17 Then God said to Noah, "Yes, this rainbow is the
sign of the covenant I am confirming with all the
creatures on earth." Genesis 9:12-17 NLT

Furthermore:

1 Then God blessed Noah and his sons and told
them, "Be fruitful and multiply. Fill the earth.
2 All the animals of the earth, all the birds of the
sky, all the small animals that scurry along the
ground, and all the fish in the sea will look on you
with fear and terror. I have placed them in your
power.

3 I have given them to you for food, just as I have
given you grain and vegetables.
4 But you must never eat any meat that still has
the lifeblood in it.
5 “And I will require the blood of anyone who
takes another person's life. If a wild animal kills a
person, it must die. And anyone who murders a
fellow human must die.
6 If anyone takes a human life, that person's life
will also be taken by human hands. For God made
human beings in his own image.
7 Now be fruitful and multiply, and repopulate the
earth.”
8 Then God told Noah and his sons,
9 “I hereby confirm my covenant with you and
your descendants,
10 and with all the animals that were on the boat
with you—the birds, the livestock, and all the wild
animals—every living creature on earth.
11 Yes, I am confirming my covenant with you.
Never again will floodwaters kill all living
creatures; never again will a flood destroy the
earth.”

12 Then God said, "I am giving you a sign of my covenant with you and with all living creatures, for all generations to come.
13 I have placed my rainbow in the clouds. It is the sign of my covenant with you and with all the earth.
14 When I send clouds over the earth, the rainbow will appear in the clouds,
15 and I will remember my covenant with you and with all living creatures. Never again will the floodwaters destroy all life.
16 When I see the rainbow in the clouds, I will remember the eternal covenant between God and every living creature on earth." Genesis 9:1-16 NLT

Please note and put to heart: "God is ready to repeat what He said before, that He wants to progress and settle later."

In the above covenant relationship, God instituted three distinct new features compared to the covenant with the Adams.

1. Don't eat anything with blood.
2. Don't shed the blood of any human, as I will require the blood from anybody who sheds the blood of another.

3. Life and property on earth would no longer be destroyed by floods (water).

- God gave a rainbow in the sky as His symbol to seal the covenant between Him and Noah.
- It is God's signature on that charter of fate that He will keep everything He promised in the covenant agreement. This was totally absent during the Edenic and Adamic eras because there was no sin in the garden. It was a period of innocence, and there was no need to do anything to remind Adam and Eve of God until the daily fellowship was broken through disobedience. The demonic action of Cain, who took the life of Abel, must have informed some aspects of the reforms in the covenant relationship with God.
- Lastly, Noah and his children were commanded to repopulate the world through the subsisting blessings of fruitfulness, multiplication, and dominion.

CHAPTER 10

POTHOLE RESURFACES

THE POST DILUVIAN EVENTS

Don't believe for a minute that we are regurgitating history here. Absolutely not. The Lord, by His Spirit, is leading us somewhere in our understanding of today. Sin has the same character from age to age.

18 The sons of Noah who came out of the boat
with their father were Shem, Ham, and Japheth.
(Ham is the father of Canaan.)
19 From these three sons of Noah came all the
people who now populate the earth.
20 After the flood, Noah began to cultivate the
ground, and he planted a vineyard.
21 One day he drank some wine he had made, and
he became drunk and lay naked inside his tent.
22 Ham, the father of Canaan, saw that his father
was naked and went outside and told his brothers.
23 Then Shem and Japheth took a robe, held it
over their shoulders, and backed into the tent to
cover their father. As they did this, they looked the
other way so they would not see him naked.

25 Then he cursed Canaan, the son of Ham: "May Canaan be cursed! May he be the lowest of servants to his relatives." Genesis 9:18-23, 25 NLT

My father of blessed memory said that a stick of a match can set anything worth billions of money ablaze. But it would take quite some me to rebuild and restore.

What's the worth of a stick of match relative to the damage it does to anything, if misused?

Let our stick of match parabolically used here be sin, and man and his dwelling, is the object of destruction struck and set ablaze by the wrong choice he made at the garden.

The post diluvian record of the state of the only family saved in the flood is quite disturbing. Bible records that Noah was a preacher of righteousness. (2 Peter 2:5).

Have you discovered that the most challenging times of a man are usually soon after the most outstanding victory?

As a preacher of righteousness, Noah must have thought that the people of the world, who were his greatest and worst enemies, had been done away with.

There was nothing more to do as there were no more sinful people to talk to and preach righteousness to. (This is my take, speaking as a man that I am)

Unknown to him, the energy used in preaching the message of righteousness, once deployed into making the ark, is now channelled into enjoying the works of his hands, drinking. To him, the rest God promised in righteousness had arrived.

God says 'No! As He said to Cain, "...Sin is crouching at the door, eager to control you. But you must subdue it and be its master." and Jesus to Peter, ... Satan has asked to sift each of you like wheat.
But I have pleaded in prayer for you, Simon that your faith should not fail..."
That's it, Cain couldn't control the sin, nor could Peter. Thank God Jesus prayed for Peter, that his faith should not fail. As for Cain, the sin got a better control of him, and that resulted in the first culpable homicide in the world.

Peter denied Jesus eventually, but when his sin found him, as his eyes touched with those of Jesus, he broke down in godly sorrow in repentance.

The temptations in your life are no different from what others experience. And God is faithful. He will not allow the temptation to be more than you can stand. When you are tempted, he will show you a way out so that you can endure. 1 Corinthians 10:13 NLT

God has a way of correcting folly in the heart of man. It is called chastisement. Sometimes, it comes by allowing you to pass through some challenging situations that will awaken the folly in you.

Trying times produce tested and good men, but good times produce feeble and weak men. On and on goes the cycle.

This is an established truth that is found in most Bible characters.

Job, Noah, Abraham, Jacob, Joseph, David, Peter, and Paul are all established cases in this regard. They were chosen servants of God who passed through difficult times and energized stronger, impacting their world in their time.

Israel as a nation, Judah as a tribe, and David's family all passed through this chastisement and test to bring the best out of them.

Chastisement is not temptation with the wrong move, but testing for the right reasons. God himself does not tempt anyone. The devil is the tempter, and he does it for all the wrong reasons: to steal, kill, and destroy. God, for every good reason, may permit it, but certainly, as the scripture under reference above reveals, He will provide a way of escape when patience has had its perfect way with it. Because the devil is a specialist in this area, God allows him to poke His children in the heart and mind, wingly or unwingly, who are falling away in error and have refused wise counsel. This is to keep them tied to the apron of hope and wisdom until they inherit the kingdom.

Le on their own, men would cross barriers like Adam and be led away on their noses to their deaths, forgetting that the earth is not their final destination. There is a river whose water does not run dry and a country whose builder and ruler are not men. Man therefore needs a guide rail to make it to the expected end.

All the servants of God mentioned above in this way passed through this tunnel, and like gold subjected to the fire, they emerged victorious, inherited a good report, and are awaiting the crown.

QUESTIONS:

1.Where did the sin that reentered the world come from?

2. Who actually was Ham in identity and character.

3. Why did Noah curse Canaan, his grandchild, and not his child, Ham, the father of Canaan, who mocked him?

To deeply reflect and receive understanding from the above questions, let's peep into the scriptures.

18 The sons of Noah who came out of the boat
with their father were Shem, Ham, and Japheth.
(Ham is the father of Canaan.)
19 From these three sons of Noah came all the
people who now populate the earth.
20 After the flood, Noah began to cultivate the
ground, and he planted a vineyard.
21 One day he drank some wine he had made, and
he became drunk and lay naked inside his tent.
22 Ham, the father of Canaan, saw that his father
was naked and went outside and told his brothers.

23 Then Shem and Japheth took a robe, held it
over their shoulders, and backed into the tent to
cover their father. As they did this, they looked the
other way so they would not see him naked.
24 When Noah woke up from his stupor, he
learned what Ham, his youngest son, had done.
25 Then he cursed Canaan, the son of Ham: "May
Canaan be cursed! May he be the lowest of
servants to his relatives." Genesis 9:18-25 NLT

From the foregoing passage, we can understand and deduce the following:

1. Noah gave birth to only three children and not any more after the flood of judgment, unlike Adam and Eve, who gave birth after the judgment of the garden, even after the death of Abel and the judgment of Cain. For everything, there is a season and a time for every purpose under the heavens. Ecclesiastes 3:1

In life, we have to understand that there will come a time when we will not be able to do certain things. We then pray to God to teach us, as scripture posits, to number our days so that we apply our hearts to wisdom, doing what we have to do as we see the daystar approaching.

2. The three children of Noah, Shem, Ham, and Japheth, populated the whole earth after the judgment.

Past generations gave way to new ones, renewing and replenishing the earth, procreating, multiplying, and spreading.

3. In the absence of sin and sinners, supposedly following the judgment on sinners, Noah busied himself with husbandry even in his old age. Age is not an excuse to do the good work assigned to you. There is no dull moment for a productive mind. We may transit from one occupation to another as the demands of each me and season face us.
4. One day he got drunk and laid naked in the tent. Many believed that this must have been after a feast at which he may have offered some sacrifices to God to thank Him, probably for a good harvest. Always thank God.
5. His younger son (probably the youngest), Ham, saw his father in that naked situation and went out in the street and told the elder ones, Shem and Japheth.

6. In response, Shem and Japheth took cloth, went backwards, looked away, and covered the nakedness of their father.
7. When Noah woke up and found out what Ham had done, he pronounced a curse on his son, Canaan, saying, "May he, Canaan, be the lowest of servants to his relatives."
8. Noah went ahead to pronounce blessings on the other two of his sons, Shem and Japheth. (To be discussed in the next chapter.) It is safe to say here that blessings will always be more plentiful and ahead of curses, even where curses seem to come first and dominate.

It is therefore clear that the pothole of sin surfaced again through Ham. He, being a father as reported, was vile in soul, attitude, character, and act, mocking a father like him and one that begat him.
Decency demands that he should exercise due honour; instead, he disobeyed. He received his just recompense, albeit not directly, but his son, Canaan, was the victim.

This indiscretion marked him out as carrying that cursed seed, which manifested in the garden and took hold of the lineage of Cain soon afterwards.

Here is why I said so:

Apart from mockery of the father, the blessed of God, and the righteous, the emphasis is on the fact that he is the father of Canaan, a characterization that was not mentioned of the elderly ones, Shem and Japheth, which would mean that he ran off first, before others, to marry, as it is common and characteristic of that cursed line.

This is evident in Cain, the champion of this evil record, who ran off before the blessed seed of Seth and started marrying and giving in marriages, building cities, and naming them after themselves, without giving God glory. (See Gen.4:16-24).

This was even before Seth, the replacement of Abel, the blessed seed, began to produce. (Gen 4:25).

Many believe that the folly displayed by Ham was probably retributive to a rebuke he must have received from the father to check his perhaps drinking spree; hence, he invited his brothers to come see the man that used to rebuke him in particular for wrongdoings. I'm considering this from a man's perspective supported by man's typical archetype.

Mischief in the heart of man has a way of being spiteful in revenge, and that which we rebuke others for could turn around and get a better part of us.

Noah was a preacher of righteousness, and the devil could target him for destruction, as he does every believer.
Let him that thinks he stands beware, lest he fall.
The Apostle Paul prayed this prayer:
But I keep it under my body and bring it into subjection, lest, by any means, when I have preached to others, I myself should be a castaway. 1 Corinthians 9:27

On the part of Noah, his indiscretion in drunkenness means that his righteousness was of integrity and sincerity of heart, not that he was without sin. No man is. We are made righteous.

The implication of this is that God looks at our hearts and not necessarily at our arts.

When our hearts are right with God, sin could pull us in and play a trick on us to push us to err. You recall the census David embarked upon that attracted the rebuke of God and resulted in the deaths of thousands of innocent Israelites? Scripture says that the Devil sponsored that project, as he did in the Garden of Eden.

In such circumstances, instant repentance restores us to our blessings, and we are never denied them, notwithstanding our error, if we turn around in repentance.

It has to be pointed out then that this sin is a dangerous pothole, one that could be covered until the underlying fault is escalated, filled, and mended permanently. How can this be achieved? Next,

CHAPTER 11

POTHOLE OF SIN RESURFACES, TAKES HOLD, SPREADS, AND DESTROYS YET AGAIN

From what played out in the foregoing chapter, it is evident that sin, both of the beast and man, was onboard the ark. After all, God commanded that even the unclean animals should be sourced and taken aboard the ship. It was sin that made them unclean. The natural man would want to query God for allowing unclean animals and evidently unclean men to be taken aboard. Nothing is hidden from him. He knows everything.

The truth is that the foolishness of God is far wiser than that of men, and His weakness is far stronger than that of the mighty. No one knows for sure why God allowed the unclean animals on the ship, even if we feign blindness about the nature of man also onboard.

This I know: The devil caused the downfall of man by using an animal in the form of a cattle that was described as very smart and subtle. So both man and animal, from what we know, are accessories to the crime against God. The Devil, the tempter, a heavenly creature in the rank of an arch angel, created as Lucifer, who even challenged God on the heavenly throne, is the wrongdoer and the ringleader.

Accordingly, man and animals are victims of their scheme and conspiracy, prey much affected like God was but certainly worse off. This is why sin wears the all-round garment of deception, because even the schemer suffers its effect since, by God's word, your sin would find you out. There's no escape route; it's just a matter of me. When it does, you suffer the consequences.

God is righteous, and it would be unfair to terminate entirely the lives of those creations of His that the devil came after to protest his banishment from heaven to the outer world.

The devil is not a match for God Almighty at any level of wit or might. God is the creator and sovereign. The devil is a creature that is dependent. He can, on his own, do nothing against God and the truth except contrive insidious schemes.

A time has been set for the full restoration of all things and the judgment of the devil, the beast, and false teachers whom the devil has hired to continue to wage war against God and anything godly in active collaboration with the kings of this earth.

1. Why are the nations so angry? Why do they
waste their time with futile plans?
2 The kings of the earth prepare for bale; the rulers
plot together against the LORD and against his
anointed one.
3 "Let us break their chains," they cry, "and free
ourselves from slavery to God."
4 But the one who rules in heaven laughs. The
Lord scoffs at them.
5 Then in anger he rebukes them, terrifying them
with his fierce fury. (Psalms 2:1-5, NLT)

A bit of history to trace the lineage of Ham, who harmed the father and incurred his wrath, albeit indirectly.

Watch!

6 The descendants of Ham were Cush, Mizraim,
Put, and Canaan.

7 The descendants of Cush were Seba, Havilah,
Sabtah, Raamah, and Sabteca. The descendants of
Raamah were Sheba and Dedan.
8 Cush was also the ancestor of Nimrod, who was
the first heroic warrior on earth.
9 Since he was the greatest hunter in the world,
his name became proverbial. People would say,
"This man is like Nimrod, the greatest hunter in the
world."
10 He built his kingdom in the land of Babylonia,
with the cies of Babylon, Erech, Akkad, and Calneh.
11 From there he expanded his territory to Assyria,
building the cities of Nineveh, Rehoboth-ir, Calah,
12 and Resen (the great city located between
Nineveh and Calah).
13 Mizraim was the ancestor of the Ludites,
Anamites, Lehabites, Naphtuhites, 14 Pathrusites,
Casluhites, and the Caphtorites, from whom the
Philisnes came.
15 Canaan's oldest son was Sidon, the ancestor of
the Sidonians. Canaan was also the ancestor of the
Hites,
16 Jebusites, Amorites, Girgashites,
17 Hivites, Arkites, Sinites,

18 Arvadites, Zemarites, and Hamathites. The
Canaanite clans eventually spread out,
19 and the territory of Canaan extended from
Sidon in the north to Gerar and Gaza in the south,
and east as far as Sodom, Gomorrah, Admah, and
Zeboiim, near Lasha.
20 These were the descendants of Ham, idenfied
by clan, language, territory, and naonal identy.
(Genesis 10:6-20, NLT)

Our objective above is to establish the concomitant appearance of the pothole of sin, which one would have thought perished in the deluge soon afterwards.

The relevance is to see the internal and dominant nature of sin, which started small in a seemingly harmless act of leaning and translated to disobedience. How it spread and became the dominant character of man and rendered him helpless, even from the one that deceived him.

THE POPULATION OF THE EARTH AFTER THE FLOOD

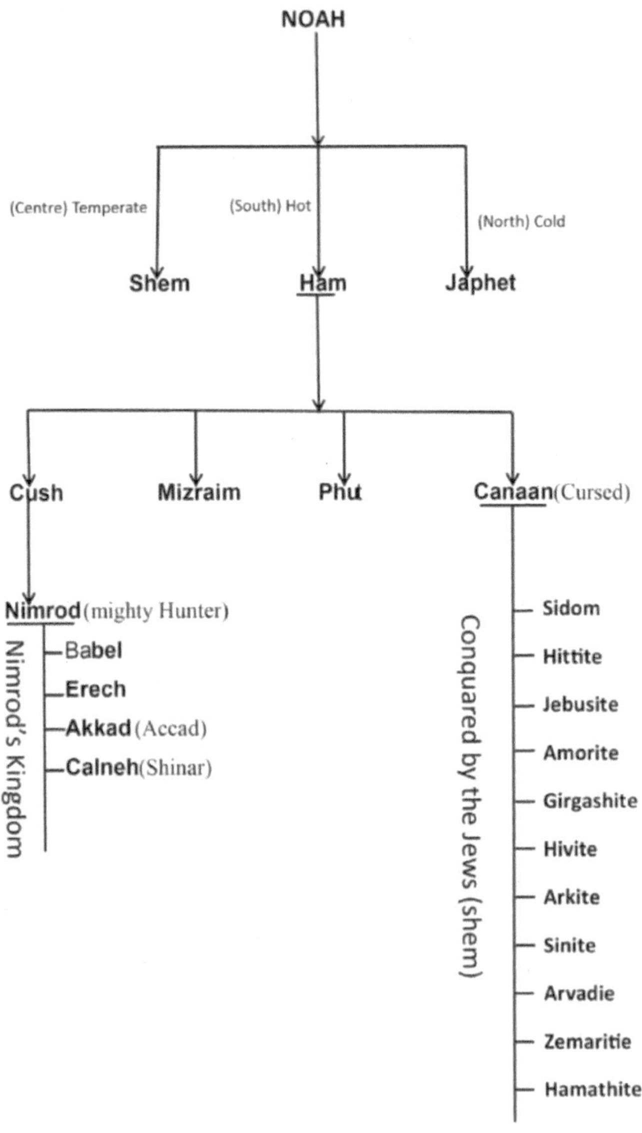

Fig.1. The family tree in posterity of Noah in post diluvian world.

Source: Configured from the Authorized King James Version by the Author.

The above posterity and family tree, like the organogram of an organization, shows the pictorial slide of the world in the post-diluvian world.

At the apex of this population tree is Noah, under whom you see his three children, Shem, Ham, and Japheth, by whom the whole world was peopled after the flood. That's in line with God's blessings pronounced on Adam and Eve and reinstated on Noah and his three children.

May the blessings of God become true and real in your life and those of your household, in the name of Jesus Christ.

But we have to be careful what we beget.

Scripture says thus:

Woe unto him that saith unto his father, What begettest thou? or to the woman, What hast thou brought forth? (Isa 45:10, KJV)

Their respective descendants are shown exactly below each child, and it is clear from the distribution on that Ham appears to be very active, energetic, populous, mobile, and definitely industrious, at least from what is visible to the eyes. What came out of him, relative to others, through Canaan that gave rise to eleven nations is massive. Does that tell you something? Hold your breath.

I am using the organogram format to present the population of the world and to make the case that man is organic in nature and is the life of any institution by which it grows in number and spreads.

We are focusing more on Ham for an obvious reason: to answer our next two questions posed in the previous chapter. This is not, however, to the exclusion of others, as doing so would deny us full view of the graces of Providence hidden in the entire picture. So we follow the Holy Spirit to lay our case and draw our lessons and/or answers to the questions before us.

1. The repopulation of the world in a post-diluvian event is undertaken in chapter 10 of the Book of Genesis.

Ten in spiritual significance means completion, full cycle, and authority or empowerment. Accordingly, this revelation, properly situated in Chapter 10, acknowledges that the world had gone through a complete cycle after the judgment and was ready for a new phase of empowerment.

Though it reopens again here on earth, standing on the saved family of Noah, according to the word and promises of God, it points in many ways to how the world it now begets will also end and give way to yet another world on the authority of God, the third in phase and series.

Watch!

26 When the Son of Man returns, it will be like it was in Noah's day.
27 In those days, the people enjoyed banquets and pares and weddings right up to the me Noah entered his boat and the flood came and destroyed them all. (Luke 17:26-27 NLT)

2. The Son of Man under reference is Jesus Christ, the Son of God. In this sense, Noah was a type of Christ, by whose favor members of his family, seven in number, were saved. Those members

of his family are like the present-day believers in Christ, who would escape the wrath of God in judgment, not necessarily because of their self-righteousness but because of the goodness, mercy, and favor of Jesus, the Son of God.

3. So beyond Noah, see Jesus and His Father, whose grace and favor saved Noah and his family, just as He raised Jesus from the grave, and ultimately those who believe in Him by boarding the ark of salvation in Christ Jesus.

The future, here foretold and represented in the story of Noah and his family, is our elevated view, figuratively.

Imagine what would have happened to any of the seven members of the family of Noah during the flood were it not for God's gesture, goodness, and kindness.

That's what would happen to anyone who rejects Jesus Christ as the Son of God, by whom God has prepared an ark to ferry to safety those who believe and remain faithful and steadfast during the impending judgment of this world, on the return of Jesus, not to save any, but to judge and rid the world of sin and wickedness. This pattern of the consequences of the choices we make based on the word of God, good or bad, would continue generation after generation. Whether it is in this very destruction of the first world, the destruction of Sodom and Gomorrah, the judgment of Korah, Jotham, and Abiram that rebelled against Moses and Aaron, or the rebellion of Israel in the desert, the sin of rejecting the word of God has consequences. Righteousness in obedience is usually and duly rewarded for upholding the word of God.

2. All through the scripture, Shem is mentioned first whenever there is reference to the three children of Noah. But in presenting this account of how the world was populated after the flood, it begins with Japhet, who is, naturally and probably, the eldest son of Noah.

Next to him is the account of Ham, who is probably the youngest son of Noah. While the account of Shem, who is mentioned first as pointed out above, is last in the presentation of the account of their descendancy in posterity.

The layout is, therefore:
Japheth: Gen. 10:2–5 (4 verses).
Ham. Gen. 10:6–20 (15 verses)
Shem. Gen. 10:21–31 (11 verses)

As usual, the cursed line is the loudest, most dominant, and seemingly the noisiest.

Keep in mind that the entire earth was bequeathed to Noah and his children in blessing, with a promise under covenant by God not to flood it again as long as it remains, though not to the exclusion of another judgment through other means.

In this case, the entire earth could be seen as an inheritance that Noah had a responsibility to divide among his three children.

Here are what lessons and spiritual wisdom we could deduce and learn from that family based on a cursory ethnological study of the above abridged family tree:

Japheth and his descendants primarily occupied and populated the world's cold northern regions. This would mean broadly (not strictly) the entire present-day Europe and Asia, and possibly North America.

Ham and his descendants peopled and predominantly occupied the hot southern part of the world, notably the African continent, especially the northern part (Egypt, Ethiopia), and the southern parts of Arab nations in the south of the middle.

Sin has consequences; it's no wonder then that Noah would reflect this truth in the area he allocates to stubborn Ham, who harmed his emotions.

Let him and his children, especially Canaan, therefore go and bale with the hot weather that tans as well as contend with the deserts. (This is speaking humanly, but remember that God had blessed the entire earth.)

For more insights on the areas involved and on these very energetic people, a special mention is made of Nimrod, probably the first son of Cush, the first son of Ham.

Three things are said about this Nimrod,
fathered by Cush, the first son of Ham. I).
He was a mighty man on earth.

Ii). He was a mighty hunter before the Lord.
iii). He built and had a kingdom, which began at Babel in the land of Shinar (Babylon).

Remember the building of the Tower of Babel told in Genesis.11, where God had to scatter them by confusing their tongues?

From the stories associated with Nimrod, which means firm, here are the things we need to know:

On a positive note, he was the grandson of Ham, who pushed the frontiers of knowledge by governing, building, ruling, subduing, multiplying, and increasing so much that he had a kingdom. This was the first me 'kingdom' appeared in the Bible associated with his name. Kingdoms are made up of domains, and domains are maintained by authorities and powers.

This means that he had a good understanding of the Adamic covenant between God and Adam and the Noahic covenant between his great-grandfather (Noah) and his great-grandfather (Ham), with respect to the blessing of multiplying and dominion of the earth and its preservation.

Secondly, these covenants expanded in the Noahic Covenant, with man granted the judicial authority to self-govern, including taking the life of any man who sheds blood innocently.

This powerful Chief of Cush ran off with this understanding, had four cities or domains to himself, making up his kingdom, and yet added another four, including Assyria, with its capital in Nineveh, on the southern side of Ancient Babylon (present-day Iran). This was probably before anybody could say Jack, and it could be an effort to prove everybody wrong that their seemingly unfavorable allocation was a disadvantage. However, the best response to God's rebuke is not arrogance under the pretense that it doesn't exist. Such pushback would always backfire, as God expects repentance in penance and not arrogant resistance.

On the negative side,

This Nimrod of a man may have pursued this agenda in a ruthless manner, brutally violating the rights of men for his personal glory and pride; hence, he was described as a mighty hunter before the Lord, which even became a proverb: "as mighty as mighty Nimrod the hunter."

To hunt, in absolute terms, means to chase down animals (games) and kill them for consumption or commercial purposes. Many think that Nimrod must have been so skilled in hunting games that he was able to rid the earth then of rampaging wild beasts that were dangers to his people after the flood, and they admired him for that.

In figurative terms, hunting means "to lie in wait" and cause bodily harm or injury, or even kill or kidnap for a purpose.

In this sense, many believe Nimrod coerced people, violated their freedom, and pushed them into the pursuit of his personal agenda, building his kingdoms.

This might be clear evidence of tyranny or dictatorship, with which he built his kingdoms and expanded them, characteristic of brutal leaders in human rights violations as we see today.

Why before the Lord?

Nimrod was pursuing this insidious agenda based on the clause in the Noahic Covenant for man to govern himself, so much so that he can judicially take the life of anyone who sheds blood unjustly. However, this was designed to be done in righteousness, on behalf of God.

Nimrod's excesses were presumed to be on account of this permission, or approval, as it were. But alas, this power was abused, and in their self-centeredness, it became obvious that men, evidently like Nimrod, governed for themselves.

The evidence of this is what happened in Babel (Shinar or Babylon), where these people gathered to build a tower to reach God and make a name for themselves. Nimrod was presumed to have spearheaded and championed that project since his kingdom started there.

God destabilized the ill-conceived project, confused their tongues, and scattered them all over the earth.

The fact that Babel, Assyria, Nineveh, and Babylon, which are all symbols of apostasy in affront to God, are associated with Nimrod, reveals the lie and hypocrisy in him to challenge God wingly or unwingly through the flesh,

He was a Cushite chief, and one of the great domains in his kingdom, the Accadians (black heads and faces), were conquered by the Semites, mainly the people of Northern Babylon (white faces).

The Accadians under Nimrod attained a level of civilization, invented the form of wring in pictorial hieroglyphics and cuneiform, and with it wrote many books on papyrus and clay.

This history links and connects them to Egypt in North Africa, where such civilization in wring was found, as well as to ancient Northern Babylon, where recently discovered mounds of what used to be the fortresses of Nebuchadnezzar, a one-me powerful Babylonian king, also linked them to the Accadians, whom they conquered.

The confusion of tongues in Babel and the scattering of these people caused them to spread up to North and East Africa, Ethiopia, many parts of the Arab peninsula, and even Persia.

The last and cursed son of Ham, Canaan, was not any less energetic, daring, or desperate. They occupied the best land in the middle. Eleven nations coming out of the cursed seed speak volumes about the desperation of the cursed in self-seeking. The curse on him was not evident in his prosperity in posterity, which bespeaks the truth that even the cursed could prosper in his wicked schemes, but to his ultimate ruin and doom. (Read Psalm 73.)

On the other hand, the lack or absence of material wealth does not, on its own, undermine or diminish the blessings of the blessed seed.

While Seth, the substitute for Abel, the blessed seed, was yet to give birth, the cursed and rejected seed, Cain, took off, married, and started building and naming cities after themselves, becoming mighty in science and technology. (Gen.4).

The seeming success in the visible material prosperity of Cain and his descendants, sing briefly in a few verses of this chapter, is nothing compared to the exploits of the blessed seed, whose posterity broke out in chapter 5, occupying the whole chapter.

All these are proofs of what the preacher says in Ecclesiastes 9:11:—I have observed something else under the sun. The fastest runner doesn't always win the race, and the strongest warrior doesn't always win the bale. The wise sometimes go hungry, and the skillful are not necessarily wealthy. And those who are educated don't always lead successful lives. It is all decided by chance, by being in the right place at the right me. (NLT)

The mingling between these two seeds, the blessed of Seth and the cursed or rejected of Cain in marriage, produced the giants that filled the earth with violence. That led to its destruction through the judgment of the flood.

In essence, it is safe to say that the Cainic spirit of acquision, building, and materialism, most often in crushing oppression of others and rebellion against God in apostasy (see Gen 4), revived in Ham as the cursed seed opposed to God. It is not clear how this came about. Possibly Ham married from that cursed seed of Cain, and his descendants, being the vilest of the three children of Noah, manifested this in his standoff against the father in mockery. That earned him and his seed, Canaan in particular, a curse by that righteous man of God, Noah (his father), for whose sake the entire family was saved, including the boldfaced Ham.

They are the worst enemies of the blessed seeds (Japhet and Shem), who are in close affinity as brothers and who cast that veil of decency on their father to cover his nakedness, even to themselves.
This makes the case that the righteous should not rejoice over sin or mock a sinner, as God might not hold them guiltless.

The rivalry between the cursed and blessed was evident in no small measure in the postdiluvian era.

We should mourn over sin and assist those under its attack to gain freedom.

The confusion of tongues at Babel was God's rebuke of man for attempting to unite to reach Him through a physical means. It was, however, in some ways a testament to man's hunger for God, attesting prophetically to the Church that would be the bond of unity of the human races in Christ for God.

That dispersal created mixed races of both the cursed and the rejected seeds, especially in the middle of the earth, where the most blessed seed, Shem, and his descendants were located, identified, separated, and preserved, surrounded by these wild descendants of Ham on all sides. (Next Chapter)

"Out of darkness, God called out light, and as the account of creation shows, it happened in the midst of chaos."

God is always in the midst, dwelling among His people.

Please get my book titled "Partake to Connect to the Power of the Holy Communion, for more on the covenants and the dispensations that underpin them and for more insights.

CHAPTER 12

GOD IN THE MIDST OF THE BLESSED ENCLOSED AND ENCUMBERED SEED

---

21 Unto Shem also, the father of all the children of
Eber, the brother of Japheth the elder, even to him
were children born.
22 The children of Shem; Elam, and Asshur, and
Arphaxad, and Lud, and Aram.
23 And the children of Aram; Uz, and Hul, and
Gether, and Mash.
24 And Arphaxad begat Salah; and Salah begat
Eber.
25 And unto Eber were born two sons: the name
of one was Peleg; for in his days was the earth
divided; and his brother's name was Joktan.
26 And Joktan begat Almodad, and Sheleph, and
Hazarmaveth, and Jerah, 27 And Hadoram, and
Uzal, and Diklah,
28 And Obal, and Abimael, and Sheba,
29 And Ophir, and Havilah, and Jobab: all these
were the sons of Joktan.

30 And their dwelling was from Mesha, as thou
goest unto Sephar a mount of the east.
31 These are the sons of Shem, after their families,
after their tongues, in their lands, after their
nations. (Gen. 10:21-31)

I am not oblivious to the fact that believers are evasive and allergic to genealogy. They believe it's a waste of their time. These same believers can sit in front of television to watch endless analysis after analysis of the Premier League, touching on every player, every game, and every move, incisively breaking it down, projecting, and drawing some conclusions. Betting is even built around such analysis and projections.

Unknown to them, there is so much packed into genealogies that they say a lot about how the world began, where it is, and where it is headed. So much that should be unpacked by the leading of the Holy Spirit, who packed them there.

That's what this is all about.

There is a principle in Bible interpretation that says "the key to the compound or house is right at the gate or door entrance, respectively". What a book, a chapter, or a verse of the Bible is all about is right at the first chapter, first verse, or first words of the book, chapter, or verse, respectively. I hope you get this.

Leveraging on this principle, the very few words of the first few verses of this section of the highlights of the posterity of Shem and his descendants say a lot about this blessed seed.

It is not clear why Moses, the writer and author of this book, decided to take on them last when they had always been mentioned first in reference to the children of Noah.

Here are possible indicators:

1. With this blessed seed, God began a separation between the blessed seed and the cursed seed for the effective conferment of the blessing promised by Noah to honor
   His word.
2. He himself, Moses, was an offspring of this very beloved seed of God, and he wanted to say more about them and their posterity, not only now but going forward.
3. As the elder by birth or by blessing, he (Shem) should have the last say: either way, the first shall be the last and the last the first, a scriptural

principle that saw Abel/Seth preferred to Cain, Isaac to Ishmael, Jacob to Esau, and the biggest of them all, Jesus, the second Adam, preferred to Adam, the first man.

4. Talking about Jesus, the promised seed under the Adamic covenant that would crush the head of the serpent that caused the fall, he, like Moses, came from this blessed seed to move the redemption agenda in the preservation of God's inheritance forward towards the manifestation of the kingdom.
5. Do you remember the tribes and those that sat at the eastern part of the Tabernacle, in the desert, during the travail of Israel? Where were Moses and Aaron always sing, and on which side of the temple was the ark of the covenant always placed? That was the symbol of Jesus in the middle. Where do you find Israel today?

Accordingly, we see this clearly indicated in the introduction of Shem and his descendants. This blessed seed, above all his brethren, occupied the middle of the earth by way of ancestral inheritance and relative to Japheth in the north and Ham in the south. However, the centre is usually the concentration of a mixed multitude of all races.

Extreme cold in the north and extreme heat in the south would force people to move to the center to avoid the two extremes. But with modern technology and civilization, those situations could be contained and managed to reduce migration. Other factors such as mismanagement and political and religious persecution now

drive immigration worries, and this is across the entire region of the world, with the western world at the receiving end.

Looking at Jesus on the cross with four Cardinal points, where do you see His heart correspondingly placed? The centre of course, is where the north, south, east, and west meet.
This is how the first four verses of the account of the posterity of Shem begin:

21 Unto Shem also, the father of all the children of
Eber, the brother of Japheth the elder, even to him
were children born.
22 The children of Shem; Elam, and Asshur, and
Arphaxad, and Lud, and Aram.
23 And the children of Aram; Uz, and Hul, and Gether,
and Mash.
24 And Arphaxad begat Salah; and Salah begat Eber.
(Genesis 10:21-24)

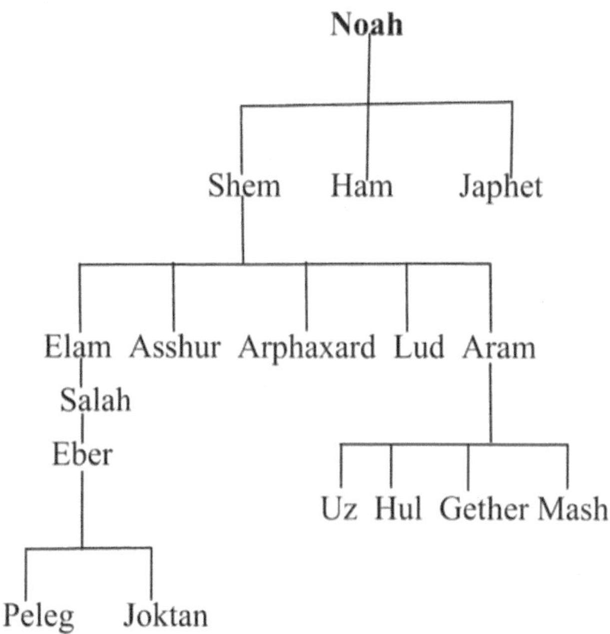

Fig 2. The Pictogram of Shem’s Posterity
Source: Configured from the Authorised King James Version by the Author.

Right at the opening, Shem was directly linked to Eber, who is his great-grandson in the third generation. The first generation starts with Elam, the second generation, followed by Uz, then Arphaxad, among the first genera on, who gave birth to Salah, the 2nd generation, and Salah begot Eber, the 3rd generation.

Here is why:

Eber is the ancestral patriarch or progenitor of the Hebrews, otherwise known as the Jews or Israelites in present-day identity.

In Luke 3:35, he is called Heber, and his name means beyond.

The addition of the Hebrew letter 'H' to his name has two spiritual implications.

1. That's how God a aches Himself to the professors of His life, like in the case of Abram, Abraham, Sarai, and Sarah, to distinguish them from those that profane

2. It also improves on the meaning of the name from "beyond" to "passing over," from which that great Sabbacal feast of dedication "Passover" derives, or better yet, derives from it meaning dedication or set apart: HOLY TO THE LORD!

Altogether, that name inspires the professors of good religion to look beyond this earth, which we are passing over, to our true home in the Kingdom of God through Jesus Christ.

In these truths, please observe how God inspires his children to be wary of the names they call anything, especially their offspring. It could ensnare or set free.

In Christ, He hid and revealed salvation, being our Saviour. (Ma.1:21)

Noah as a name means 'rest' or 'comfort, prophetically given to him by his father.
Lamech (Gen. 5:29), seeking rest or a break from the suffering of man arising from the curse of the land by God for the sake of Adam's sin, means 'needy man.

Salah followed this divine order and named his son Eber, meaning beyond their time and ahead to Passover and all the troubles of this life on earth.

He is therefore a peculiar professor of good religion who did not participate, most probably, in the affront in the building of the Babel at Shinar to challenge God. His own name, Salah, means 'shoot'.

Eber or Heber too, prophetically named his own first son 'Peleg' in the 4th generation.

Peleg means 'division', by which it could be understood that God answered his prayers by making a division between him and his people (now the Hebrews), out of which that great patriarch Abraham, a great professor of good religion and friend of God, descended. He became the father of the Hebrews as a people and a nation.

Genesis 10:25 And unto Eber were born two sons: the name of one was Peleg; for in his days was the earth divided; and his brother's name was Joktan.

God, out of the woolly bunch of the human race, pulled out a single and tiny rill or thread to preserve the seed of the woman, which would accomplish His will in the redemption of mankind from the sin of self-centeredness and apostasy.

Have you separated yourself from this wicked world, or are you sll part and parcel of it?

How far do you see yourself separated from the whole world, not physically but in the adoption, practice, and participation of world systems, under the influence of the devil?

In whom do you feel safe and preserved: in Christ and the promises of God in Him, or in your efforts, connections, and/or security arrangements and wealth?

Watch!

17 Wherefore come out from among them, and be
ye separate, saith the Lord, and touch not the
unclean thing; and I will receive you,
18 And will be* a Father unto you, and ye shall be
my sons* and daughters, saith the Lord Almighty.
(2 Corinthians 6:17-18, KJV)

14. I have given them thy word; and the world
hath hated them, because they are not of the
world, even as I am not of the world.
15. I pray not that thou shouldest take them out
of the world, but that thou shouldest keep them
from the evil.

16. They are not of the world, even as I am not of the world.
17. Sanctify them through thy truth: thy word is truth. (John 17:14-17, KJV)

The second grace observable in the Mega Charter of Shem and his posterity is his link to Japheth, who probably is the first natural son of Noah but is not explicitly evident in the introduction.
To Shem also, the father of all the children of Eber, the brother of Japheth the elder, were born children. (Genesis 10:21)

Whether Shem is the elder or Japheth, what is not in denial is that both are described as brothers, to the exclusion of impudent Ham, who threw himself on the ground. Of course, that is not causeless, but must surely have arisen because it was justified.
Ham was as much a brother to both Shem and Japheth, both of whom are not recognized here beyond the safety of the flood.
On the contrary, and to elevate the spiritual importance of this assertion, Ham is described as the father of Canaan, the cursed seed (Gen. 9:18–22).

We know them by their fruits. If success has many brethren, failure too is not barren.

What has light got to do with darkness?

Both of them, Shem and Japheth, received a blessing from Noah, their father, apparently as a reward for their good judgment when they refused to mock their father (Noah), instead honouring him and covering his nakedness.
Japheth means wide spreading, by the enlargement of God. (Gen 9:27). Some translate this to mean God will make him beautiful," hence they are "whites' ' as opposed to the Hamic, who are black in their faces and heads, as in Cushites and Accadians.

The blackness, which is the natural consequence of the sun's heat because they are located in the south, could also be figuratively indicative of the state of their hearts in pursuit of things of this world with darkened souls, faces, and heads.

The prophetic blessings on Japheth are largely fulfilled in the sense that upon the earth, the descendants of Japheth populated Europe and a larger part of Asia (except perhaps the Western part), plus possibly America. It is a known fact that government, science, technology, architecture, etc. are in their best forms and origins found in the areas peopled by this blessed seed: Europe and America, with presence in other

parts of the world, streaming and looming large, both in land mass and population.
They are, however, described as heathens, meaning non-Hebrews or non-Israelites. Noah prophesied that Japheth would dwell in the tent of Shem, while Canaan would be a servant to both. Nobody knows the exact track on which God will fulfil this prophecy.

It is, however, noticeable that there is great affinity between the Hebrews and America, plus some parts of Asia and Europe, in what has become an Indo-European grouping of human races based on recent ethnological science studies.

Ultimately, we also know that Christ Jesus said that the Jews would and are united with the gentile nations (mainly the Japhetic) to become the Church. The head of that church, we know, is Jesus Christ, in whom God has prepared a large tent to accommodate everybody, including the gentiles or heathens (any nation other than Israel) for the blessing of eternal life that Noah and his three children previewed and foreshadowed.

Remember, it was the joint gracious manner of wisdom employed by Shem and Japheth in covering the nakedness of their father Noah that earned them those profound blessings of their father.

On the other hand, the despicable, deplorable, and abhorable insolence Ham meted to the father of righteousness by God's pronouncement earned him and his descendants the curse that staged them against God and his favour.

Over all, please understand and know in your heart what God personally revealed to me in this study that you might not find elsewhere:

1. Noah did not have three children by accident. They are pictures of the three phases the world would pass through before everything would merge into one, resulting in the third phase, which is the Kingdom of God.
2. One phase is gone already; the second is presently streaming and running, being a mixture of the good, the bad, and the ugly. The present generation
3. The final, previewed in the blessings of Shem, will have the kingdoms of Japheth, who is blessed with the blessings of the earth, flow into the Church, which is the tent God has provided to accommodate all believers with Jesus as the head, in the Kingdom of God that will result from it.

Furthermore, please understand how this plays out in what those three children did to their father, Noah. The garment Shem and Japheth cast on the nakedness of their father is reflective of the covering God made of the nakedness of Adam and Eve with the skin of an animal and prophetic of the garment of righteousness He casts on us through His Son, Jesus Christ, to atone for our sins. God does not see sin. He has the purest eyes.

On the contrary, Ham is a picture of the devil, who mocks, makes jest of, and exposes sin to his peril, just as the devil did in the garden.

The blessing of Japheth reflects earthly blessings in beauty and wealth, which will not glory in the presence of God, while that of Shem is heavenly, pointing to one, Our Lord Jesus. That is why Noah did not bless Shem directly, but God, for him (an indirect blessing). But Japheth was blessed with earthly posterity (directly).

The most enduring blessing you can bequeath to your children is the blessing of God in salvation. Dedicate them to God in Christ. It doesn't preclude them from receiving and having earthly material blessings.

Canaan will serve both of them, subjugated to the authority of the two

Watch!

26. And he said, Blessed be the LORD God of Shem; and Canaan shall be his servant.

27. God shall enlarge Japheth, and he shall dwell in the tents of Shem; and Canaan shall be his servant.

28. And Noah lived after the flood three hundred and fifty years.

29. And all the days of Noah were nine hundred and fifty years: and he died. (Gen 9:26-29, KJV)

CHAPTER 13

FIXING THE POTHOLE OF SIN IN MORALITY, CHARACTER AND DESTINY

CONTEMPORARY LIFE ISSUES.

In the course of this project, news broke in my country, Nigeria, of a teenage student in one of the states who manipulated her Joint Admission and Matriculation Board result. When she was caught, with a bold face, she did a live video of herself, claiming she was, at her age, incapable of manipulating her own result. She was holding and displaying to the whole world a computer printout of her result, purportedly printed from the website of the exam body. It was later discovered that she skilfully forged that result properly in pursuit of a price tag of three million naira, promised by the managing director of a business organization in her state. The prize was to be given to the highest scorer in the entrance exam to go to college in Nigeria.

When the investigation revealed and confirmed that she forged the result, she broke down and was reeling in shame, especially as she was barred from participating in the exam for three years. Her score was also withdrawn and cancelled.

Earlier in yet another case in a neighbouring state of this young teenager, a former high-ranking member of Parliament was jailed with his wife and family doctor in the United Kingdom for attempting to harvest the kidney organ of a young boy, who obviously was an accessory to the crime but raised alarm when the deal failed, and he was to be deported to Nigeria.

All these were happening when young teenage Nigerians were making waves all over the world, graduating as the best students in China, the United States, the United Kingdom, Cyprus, Turkey, and even neighbouring countries like Ghana and other African countries, carting away prizes, and in some cases, being chosen to deliver the graduation speech.

Talk about a mixed bag of juvenile delinquency and excellence.
Now what are the motivations for all these? They are as varied as there are cases. The diverse nature of these cases and the fact that parents are, in most cases, accessory to these crimes tell you of the infallibility and inviolability of the word of God.

Some are like the case of sponsoring your children to a wild party and then turning around to perform sacrifices in case they cursed God in their hearts. Talk about a thief giving testimony in a place of worship after a 'successful' operation.

Direct your children onto the right path, and when they are older, they will not leave it. (Proverbs 22:6 NLT)

Direct or train your children in the right path, presupposes that the director knows the right path, for no-one can give what he does not have.
The just man walketh in his integrity: his children are blessed after him. (Proverbs 20:7, KJV)

Even a child is known by his doings, whether his work be pure, and whether it be right. (Proverbs 20:11, KJV)

Foolishness is bound in the heart of a child; but the rod of correction shall drive it far from him. (Proverbs 22:15, KJV)

Withhold not correction from the child: for if thou beatest him with the rod, he shall not die. (Proverbs 23:13, KJV)

The rod and reproof give wisdom: but a child le to himself bringeth his mother to shame. (Proverbs 29:15, KJV)

INSTITUTIONS THAT FACILITATE AND SHAPE THE TRAINING OF A CHILD FOR A SANE SOCIETY IN THEIR ADOLESCENCE.

1. The Family
2. The Community
3. The Church
4. The Schools (Primary, Secondary, Tertiary)
5. The Government or Nation.

It would be foolhardy to make a full case to answer the moral and character decadence in society today. However, here is an attempt to unify our thoughts and direct them to what I believe to be the central message in this discourse.

What is true to me might not be true to you, and that's not surprising because it depends on our definitions of truth.

That debate can go on forever, and everybody would want to hold on to and stick to his point of view, driven by his teachings and experiences.

What may not be debatable, I believe, is that man does not and cannot, in his fallen state, define truth.

Given the opportunity, he would reflect his sinful nature and experiences tainted with sin in his definition to justify himself.

Consequently, someone, most certainly higher than man in knowledge, wisdom, and understanding, possesses the capacity to not just define truth but also show us what or who He is. In that case, truth is synonymous with deity, a divine being with total capacity to do anything and everything and undo them as He pleases in His sovereignty.

Even at that, we may run into yet another brick wall, trying to figure out and agree on who this person is. This is because many believe that they can make their own god, so we end up having as many gods as there are debates and perspectives reflecting diverse cultures. This debate is also not the focus of this project.

Let us take note, it's clear that the truth is a person with a personality. So is the opposite of truth, which is a lie. The truth is also given and not made up. There is no middle ground between truth and lies.

Consequently, there are only two personalities in the whole universe. Every other thing—people, nature, lifestyles, desires, pursuits, walks, work, relationships, etc.—takes after these two personalities. You are either for the truth or for the lie. You are either true or a lie. Put in another way, you either accept or reject the truth. You either speak the truth or lie, believe the truth or doubt it, live truthfully or live in lies.

Whichever you choose, wingly or unwingly, the truth is that either way, there are consequences. The truth can be found, heard, and believed.

Here are some questions you need to answer if you want to find the truth, hear it, and believe it.

1. Do you accept that you are a man (notwithstanding the gender), created, and not the creator?
2. Do you accept that, as a man, you admit you need help not just to get by but to get through, over and above this world, to inherit your inheritance?
3. Do you accept that there is a creator who created you and gave you life?
4. Do you accept that man heard and believed a report (lie) other than the given report (truth) and departed from the way (truth), followed the lie, and headed for destruction?
5. Do you accept that by believing and following a lie, man lost his true identity and took on the nature of a lie that disinherited him of his true identity?

If your answers to the above questions are in the affirmative, which I pray they are, here is the good news: the God who created you gave you a good report, that you were created in His image after His likeness, and that you started your journey until it was cut short by lies.

6 Jesus told him, "I am the way, the truth, and the life. No one can come to the Father except through
me.
7 If you had really known me, you would know who my Father is. From now on, you do know him and have seen him!" (John 14:6-7 NLT)

That's it, right there, staring at you. I mean "truth" in the middle of the three mystery words in metaphors.
I am the way, I am the truth, and I am the life.
Jesus did not say, I am a way, but the way, because there is no other way; every other way is a way that leads to destruction. He is the truth; any other speech that contradicts Him is a lie. Let all men be liars, and Jesus be true. He is the life, not a life. Any life lived without Him is in danger of hellfire because it's not the true life.

If Jesus, the truth, is not at the centre of your being, actions, decisions, choices, desires, and pursuits, you have missed the way and may lose your life unless something happens before He returns.

Earlier, before He made this assertion to Philip in particular and the disciples generally, Jesus' route revealed Him as God. Watch!

1 In the beginning the Word already existed. The Word
was with God, and the Word was God.
2 He existed in the beginning with God.
3 God created everything through him, and nothing
was created except through him.
4 The Word gave life to everything that was created,
and his life brought light to everyone.
5 The light shines in the darkness, and the darkness
can never extinguish it.
14 So the Word became human and made his home
among us. He was full of unfailing love and
faithfulness. And we have seen his glory, the glory of
the Father's one and only Son.
(John 1:1-5, 14 NLT)

CROSS REFERENCE TO PROVE THE ABOVE REVELATION:

1 In the beginning God created the heaven and the earth.

2 The earth was formless and empty, and darkness covered the deep waters. And the Spirit of God was hovering over the surface of the waters.

3 Then God said, "Let there be light," and there was light.

4 And God saw that the light was good. Then he separated the light from the darkness.

5 God called the light "day" and the darkness "night." And evening passed and morning came, marking the first day.

6 Then God said, "Let there be a space between the waters, to separate the waters of the heavens from the waters of the earth."

9 Then God said, "Let the waters beneath the sky flow together into one place, so dry ground may appear." And that is what happened.

14 Then God said, "Let lights appear in the sky to separate the day from the night. Let them be signs to mark the seasons, days, and years. (Genesis 1:1-6, 9, 14 NLT)

You see, God used His creative word, which is Jesus, to create the whole heaven and earth. Jesus is that Word

which later manifested as a human being and came to dwell among men.
Jesus is also that light that was first created, figuratively. But know that Jesus was not created; He was born as a son and as a child. (Isaiah 9)

The Light gave Life (more abundant life and eternal life) to men through the redemption plan to impart the life of God to men for the salvation of their souls after the fall in the garden.

Unfortunately, His own people, the Jews to whom He was sent, rejected Him and all He was to be to them: Way, Truth, and Life.

10 He came into the very world he created, but the world didn't recognize him.
11 He came to his own people, and even they rejected him.
12 But to all who believed him and accepted him, he gave the right to become children of God.
13 They are reborn—not with a physical birth resulting from human passion or plan, but a birth that comes from God. (John 1:10-13 NLT).
The rejection has consequences. NEXT

CHAPTER 14

THE MORALITY AND CHARACTER QUESTIONS- MORE INSIGHTS

The Wikipedia Online dictionary defines morality as follows:

(uncountable) Recognition of the distinction between good and evil or between right and wrong; respect for and obedience to the rules of right conduct; the mental disposition or characteristic of behaving in a manner intended to produce morally good results.

(countable) A set of social rules, customs, traditions, beliefs, or practices which specify proper, acceptable forms of conduct.

(countable) A set of personal guiding principles for conduct or a general noon of how to behave, whether respectable or not.

Character on the other hand is defined by the same English dictionary as follows:

- (*uncountable*) Strength of mind; resolution; independence; individuality; moral strength. *He has a great deal of character.*

- (*countable*) A unique or extraordinary individual; a person characterized by peculiar or notable traits, especially charisma.

From the above, we can relate morality to character and see their meeting point. . Following a set of rules and willingly subjecting oneself to their governance, which constitutes morality, provides you with moral fortitude within your identity, known as character.

Morality or values therefore determine and drive character, making the person unique.

Example: It's great morality not to lie, cheat, manipulate, or steal. These will combine to give the one observing those sets of moral and divine rules the unique character of a true Christian, or a great personality.

Your personality is a reference to your character based on the moral values you choose to live by, which makes you different and unique. It could be positive or negative, poor or great, depending on the perception of the person making the judgment.

For example, if I choose not to eat pork or party, that could be great or poor, depending on who you talk to.

There are, however, universal values that should regulate and serve as acceptable norms that everybody should accept in order to relate well with others.

But where can we find this golden stick that will serve as our guide?

Let's see if an answer can be found in our discourse here.

WHY DID JESUS COME TO THE EARTH?

After the fall of man, God judged man and serpent with a resolve to create enmity between the offspring of the woman (Eve in her representative capacity as mother of all living) and the offspring of the serpent, the ring leader, and all those that would follow his steps.

That's the separation of light from darkness He spoke about in Gen 1:3, and the light that manifested to give life to all creation, including man. John 1: 4

As already revealed in the last chapter, Jesus is that light, but more importantly, that seed or offspring of the woman promised in Gen. 3:15 that will crush the head of the serpent and his seed that caused the fall of man.

Like an Olympic torch packed in a secure box with maximum security and passed through all the participating countries before arriving at the venue of the country chosen for the ground finale, God packaged Jesus as that precious seed and passed Him through eight distinct covenants, from generation after generation, to carry out this peculiar and onerous task of redemption.

The fifth of those eight covenants is the Mosaic Covenant.

The Mosaic Covenant is a set of moral rules or laws that God rolled out to be observed by the Israelites in order to earn salvation. These laws enshrined in the 20th chapter of the book of Exodus, issued at Mount Sinai or Horeb, were God's response to them when they ignorantly or arrogantly rejected God's gracious offer of salvation under the Abrahamic covenant that preceded this Mosaic Covenant.

(Please get my book titled "Partake and Connect the Power in the Holy Communion, a very incisive resource on covenants.)

Rather than deliver salvation to the Israelites, the law delivered condemnation and death to them, as none could keep or meet the just requirements of the laws, which were good and holy.

This was because the law was not designed to deliver salvation to them, but to reveal their sinful state and nature and arouse their need for God in them.

That which was supposed to deliver the life of God to them ministered death to them as they kept falling short of the demands of the law.

The law was also to discipline and keep them in check until God's original plan to deliver salvation by grace through faith in His Son, Jesus to whom the promise as the seed was made, manifested.

Their rejection of grace through faith, offered through the Abrahamic covenant, could not and cannot change the plan of God, Who had made all things beautiful in His own me.

QUESTIONS:

1. In these days of coming together as a group, especially in what has come to be popular as "WhatsApp Group" on social media, how often do members of such groups respect and obey the rules of engagement?

2. Who made those rules, and why are they easily flouted despite the avowed sanctions?
3. How often do laws dissuade people from crossing the red line to violate their responsibilities?
4. Why do you think that the prisons of all the nations of the world are filled with lawbreakers?
5. Are you an oath keeper or a truce breaker, and what do you recommend as solutions to the incessant breaking of laws?

Jesus fulfilled the laws and released a template for salvation, pointing to himself.

CHAPTER 15

THE NEW TEMPLATE FOR ACQUIRING ROBUST MORALITY AND SIN RESISTANT SPIRIT IN CHARACTER

THE BEATITUDES.

When Jesus graced the earth in pursuit of the plans and purposes of God, one would have thought that He would lecture the Israelites on the content of the moral laws of God encapsulated in the Ten Commandments. No!

Instead, He showed them why they could not fulfil the laws or meet the righteous requirements of those holy codes.

This could help us answer some of the questions posed in the immediate chapter.

Their hearts were not right. The cancer of sin had defiled and corrupted them.

Like viruses in a computer, the hardware (their hearts) could not read and play the software (the moral codes of God in those laws), as they were incompatible.

The heart, therefore, needed to be reformatted by grace and reconfigured with faith. A system upgrade was imperative if the job of receiving wisdom in order to make it to the Kingdom of God was desired by anyone.

The old hard disk (the sin-ridden and hardened heart of man) was to be replaced with a new, reconfigured heart of flesh to enable it to read the mind of God. Watch!

My flesh and my heart faileth: but God is the strength of my heart, and my portion forever. (Psalms 73:26, KJV)

And I will give them one heart, and I will put a new spirit within you; and I will take the stony heart out of their flesh, and will give them a heart of flesh: (Ezekiel 11:19, KJV).

That was why Jesus went straight for the heart of men in His Sermon on the Mount.

1 One day as he saw the crowds gathering, Jesus
went up on the mountainside and sat down. His
disciples gathered around him,
2 and he began to teach them.
3 "God blesses those who are poor and realize
their need for him, for the Kingdom of Heaven is
theirs.
4 God blesses those who mourn, for they will be
comforted.
5 God blesses those who are humble, for they will
inherit the whole earth.
6 God blesses those who hunger and thirst for
justice, for they will be satisfied.
7 God blesses those who are merciful, for they will
be shown mercy.
8 God blesses those whose hearts are pure, for
they will see God.
9 God blesses those who work for peace, for they
will be called the children of God.
10 God blesses those who are persecuted for
doing right, for the Kingdom of Heaven is theirs.
11 "God blesses you when people mock you and
persecute you and lie about you and say all sorts
of evil things against you because you are my
followers. (Mathew 5:1-11, NLT)

There are nine of those beatitudes. Nine (9) is the number of fruitfulness or an ongoing life path. A baby stays nine months in the womb and continues life thereafter.

Nine (9) is also the number of decisions and judgments. Jesus healed ten, and only one (1) decided to return to thank Him, while nine (9) walked away.

The fruits of the Holy Spirit are nine (9), but technically taught as 1 + 8 (meaning that it is one and the one gives birth to eight). (More on this later.)
Jesus reflected these spiritual truths in those nine beatitudes.

The first one, and the principal, denotes humility and acceptance that one needs help because he is poor in spirit. A poor spirit needs to be reengineered to plant a new software of the Spirit of God that will accommodate His Kingdom, even in this wicked world.

It was not until Enos (meaning "man"), the son of Seth, the righteous seed, was born and named that people began to call upon the name of the Lord.
Spiritual rebirth and revival begin when you acknowledge that you are poor in spirit, needy, and

destitute (not of material things) and that help should be sent your way.

Watch!

And to Seth, to him also there was born a son; and he called his name Enos: then began men to call upon the name of the LORD. (Genesis 4:26, KJV)

And a vision appeared to Paul in the night; There stood a man of Macedonia, and prayed him, saying, Come over into Macedonia, and help us. (Acts 16:9, KJV).

Have you yet called on Him to send help to you, or do you think you can handle it? You are invited:

28. Come unto me, all ye that labour and are heavy laden, and I will give you rest.
29. Take my yoke upon you, and learn of me; for I am meek and lowly in heart: and ye shall find rest unto your souls.
30. 30. For my yoke is easy, and my burden is light. (Mat 11:28-30, KJV)

The last three of those nine beatitudes give an indication that it would take courage to come forward and accept this new spirit because it would be attacked, resisted, and pushed back against by the kingdom of darkness, even manifesting as light.

However, those who would receive the graces implanted in these beatitudes would rejoice because of what they stand for. They would be blessed wholly and deeply by a robust, enduring spiritual rebirth and revival beyond this earth, with assurance of salvation and redemption.

The greatest enemy of this spirit is the sense of the law. (This is a topic for another project.) Suffice it to say that that's the heaven-laden burden Jesus referred to in that universal invitation made to the whole world in Ma 11:28.

It is therefore important to underscore the point that Jesus and these teachings were not about filling our heads with the notions of the teachings but about receiving His Spirit, which embodies these teachings.

That was the methodology under the law, where you have professors of legalistic religion whose hearts are far removed from the graces of those laws.

It was not surprising, therefore, that it did not take root and made them even more vulnerable to the devil, who seized the law and wrecked havoc on them.

God then made a decision.

Watch!

8 But when God found fault with the people, he
said: "The day is coming, says the LORD, when I will
make a new covenant with the people of Israel and
Judah.
9 This covenant will not be like the one I made with
their ancestors when I took them by the hand and
led them out of the land of Egypt. They did not
remain faithful to my covenant, so I turned my
back on them, says the LORD .
10 But this is the new covenant I will make with
the people of Israel on that day, says the LORD : I
will put my laws in their minds, and I will write
them on their hearts. I will be their God, and they
will be my people.

11 And they will not need to teach their neighbors,
nor will they need to teach their relatives, saying,
'You should know the LORD .' For everyone, from
the least to the greatest, will know me already.

12 And I will forgive their wickedness, and I will
never again remember their sins."
13 When God speaks of a "new" covenant, it
means he has made the first one obsolete. It is now
out of date and will soon disappear. (Hebrews 8:8-13, NLT)

You heard it right. That's directly from the God of all creation.

It's no longer me to fill our heads with knowledge while the heart is barren with the truth because the Spirit of God is absent.

When you receive Jesus as your Lord and Saviour, this Spirit comes into you to dwell in you and continue to lead and teach you God's way, which is Christ in you, the hope of glory.

Watch!

16 "For this is how God loved the world: He gave
his one and only Son, so that everyone who
believes in him will not perish but have eternal life.
17 God sent his Son into the world not to judge the
world, but to save the world through him.
18 "There is no judgment against anyone who
believes in him. But anyone who does not believe

in him has already been judged for not believing in God's one and only Son. (John 3: 16-18, NLT)

9 The one who is the true light, who gives light to
everyone, was coming into the world.
10 He came into the very world he created, but
the world didn't recognize him.
11 He came to his own people, and even they
rejected him.
12 But to all who believed him and accepted him,
he gave the right to become children of God.
13 They are reborn—not with a physical birth
resulting from human passion or plan, but a birth
that comes from God.
(John 1:9-13, NLT)

How do you achieve this empowerment?

5 For Moses writes that the law's way of making a
person right with God requires obedience to all of
its commands.
6 But faith's way of getting right with God says,
“Don't say in your heart, 'Who will go up to
heaven?' (to bring Christ down to earth).
7 And don't say, 'Who will go down to the place of
the dead?' (to bring Christ back to life again).”

8 In fact, it says, "The message is very close at
hand; it is on your lips and in your heart." And that
message is the very message about faith that we
preach:
9 If you openly declare that Jesus is Lord and
believe in your heart that God raised him from the
dead, you will be saved.
10 For it is by believing in your heart that you are
made right with God, and it is by openly declaring
your faith that you are saved.
11 As the Scriptures tell us, "Anyone who trusts in
him will never be disgraced." (Rom.10:511, NLT)

WHAT HAPPENS TO YOU WHEN YOU CONFESS JESUS AS YOUR LORD AND SAVIOUR?

16 So we have stopped evaluating others from a
human point of view. At one me we thought of
Christ merely from a human point of view. How
differently we know him now!
17 This means that anyone who belongs to Christ
has become a new person. The old life is gone; a
new life has begun!
18 And all of this is a gift from God, who brought
us back to himself through Christ. And God has
given us this task of reconciling people to him.

19 For God was in Christ, reconciling the world to
himself, no longer counting people's sins against
them. And he gave us this wonderful message of
reconciliation.
20 So we are Christ's ambassadors; God is making
his appeal through us. We speak for Christ when
we plead, “Come back to God!”
21 For God made Christ, who never sinned, to be
the offering for our sin, so that we could be made
right with God through Christ. (1Cor.5: 16-21, NLT).

Here are the things to hold on to in all the Scriptures above:

1. Under the Old Testament law of seven covenants, God entered into covenant relationships with man in order to make him right with him and deliver an everlasting kingdom to him. The foretaste of this promise is the earth God bequeathed to man to inhabit.
2. None of those could deliver the kingdom to man because of sin that was yet to be conclusively dealt with and the law that sabotaged it.
3. God now sent His Son, Jesus Christ, to fulfill the law, take it out of the way of salvation, and

deliver the kingdom to those who believe, receive, and confess Him as His Son.

4. Jesus did, under a new covenant arrangement that was launched through His death on the cross and man submitting himself to that covenant.
5. From the me of His death and resurrection until He returned to firmly and conclusively establish the kingdom of His Father, sin lost its grip on those who signed on to the new covenant of grace and truth that came through His Son to enjoy eternal peace with God.
6. These people who sign on to the new covenant, the one and only one in the New Testament, are called believers; sin has no power over them because the Spirit of God in them through the blood of Jesus Christ, shed on the cross and received by faith, is sin virus resistant and robust in opposition to it.
7. Because of their decision to believe and receive the gospel, the good news, their sins are washed and forgiven, their curses reversed, and they are admitted as members of the body of Christ, the Church, as new creations:

Those who reject Jesus and the new covenant would be judged under the old covenant of the law of sin and death, and because it's clear no man can meet the righteous requirements of the law, they have no part in the new kingdom, as Jesus is the only path to it.

8. Your journey to the new kingdom under the New Covenant therefore starts with Jesus, whether you are Jew or Gentile, wise or foolish, male or female. To them, sin is not imputed because Jesus paid in full, even if they mistakenly fall into sin, as long as they are not living in sin. Amen.

RECEIVING JESUS AS LORD AND SAVIOUR HAS TWO IMPLICATIONS ON EARTH.

The first is that you receive His Spirit, which comes to dwell in you and live among the believers to help them lead a victorious Christian life. This spirit answers the moral question. That's why Jesus started with those 9 Beatitudes, targeting the heart.

Those beatitudes are not attitudinal, though they will deliver a singular attitude of godliness that you can't behave your way into.

They are spiritual, and you must receive them by faith, for them to work supernaturally in you. Your senses can neither comprehend, analyse, nor control it; it controls you.

The second outcome, or effect, is that the Spirit births nine fruits in you, which answers the question of character.

A Christian character is just one, as God is one. It is called love.

Once you have love (God), then love will deliver the other eight fruits of joy: peace, patience, goodness, kindness, meekness, faith, temperance, or self-control.

Without love, even faith cannot work, and you can't walk in love without the Spirit of love, the Holy Spirit, and you can't have the Holy Spirit without Jesus Christ, and you can't have Jesus Christ without hearing the gospel, the good news, and confessing with your mouth that Jesus is the Son of God and believing in your heart that He was raised from the dead.

With our hearts, we believe in righteousness, and with our mouths, confession is made for salvation. (Already shared above in Romans 10.)

22 But the Holy Spirit produces this kind of fruit in our lives: love, joy, peace, patience, kindness, goodness, faithfulness,
23 gentleness, and self-control. There is no law against these things!
24 Those who belong to Christ Jesus have nailed the passions and desires of their sinful nature to his cross and crucified them there. (Gal.5: 22-25)

Notice that in all the scriptures quoted in respect of this new order, Jesus, the Son of God, gave clear indications that there will be kingdoms that will stand in opposition to the true kingdom.

QUESTION

Where do you stand? Are you for or against the kingdom? Would you want to make a decision now and save yourself and your household from the impending wrath of God on the children of disobedience?

Please head to **"Faith Dedication Page "at the end of chapter 20** to dedicate your life to God through His Son, Jesus Christ, and secure a place in the spotless and pothole-free kingdom of God by grace through Jesus Christ.

When you compare the revelations the Lord, by His Spirit, has revealed and shared with us in the above chapter, they are like a research project.

In the previous chapters, we have moved from hypotheses to establishing a law.

Not law as a set of rules and regulations to observe and be regulated with from outside to give man a strength of unique character, but a law of the Spirit of life in Christ Jesus that ends the law of sin and death. Jesus is Lord.

Check the laws or constitutions of over 90% of the nations of the world; they are rooted in the biblical moral codes of the Ten Commandments and their derivatives called charges. Yet these nations are filled with criminals, both for misdemeanours and heinous crimes.

The answer lies in all we have discussed in the preceding chapter.

Separate yourself, receive Jesus Christ as your Lord and Saviour, and you will not fulfil the lust of the flesh but be led by the Spirit of God as a Son of God. Amen.

CHAPTER 16

THE GREATEST THREATS TO CIVILITY IN MORALITY AND

SPIRIT-LED CHARACTER ACROSS BOARD

When I got to this point, the Lord asked me a question. He asked me, What was the greatest challenge Jesus had in introducing the new kingdom?

I know that most of us would say sin, or moving closer and closer nearer, the Pharisees (those too far, that they can't see), the Sadducees (their counterparts, who were too sad, that they were blinded to see), and of course the Scribes (the scribblers, holding on to their scripts), but refused to listen to the author who handed down the true script.

All those are fair enough answers, but they are mere shadows, just as the concept upon which they were acting.
The apostle Paul gave us insight. Hear him:

1. Dear brothers and sisters, the longing of my heart and my prayer to God is for the people of Israel to be saved.
2. I know what enthusiasm they have for God, but it is misdirected zeal.

3. For they don't understand God's way of making people right with himself. Refusing to accept God's way, they cling to their own way of getting right with God by trying to keep the law.

4. For Christ has already accomplished the purpose for which the law was given. As a result, all who believe in him are made right with God. (Romans 10:1-4, NLT)

You see, I am sure you heard it right—clear and loud—that Christ is the end of the law, to bring righteousness to everyone who believes.

But they had a zeal to hold on to the law, while Jesus is saying, I have done it. The debt has been settled; all you need to do is ensure that you don't go back to those lifestyles that deceived you and made you vulnerable, and give thanks for what I have done for you.

Certainly, all the critiques, attacks and oppositions against Christ and His teachings, and that of His precursor, John, advocating for a change of heart, were aimed at upholding the prevailing legal system.

But as you have heard in the scripture above, "Christ is the end of the law" for all those that believe. For those who do not believe, the law remains in force, and where anyone fails in any, he has failed in all and would be adjudged to be in unbelief, which would be visited with God's wrath.

Paul, who reported this truth was the evangelist who persecuted the Christians before converting to Christianity. He was then known as Saul of Tarsus, a zealous Pharisee, zealous for keeping the law. He wanted to destroy the followers of Jesus, whom he considered to be heretics. But while on his way to Damascus to arrest more Christians, he had a vision of Jesus, who asked him, "Saul, Saul, why do you persecute me?" (Acts 9:4). This encounter changed his life and he became a believer and a preacher of the gospel.

In that regard, the greatest threat to salvation by faith is the brazen activities of fake teachers and false prophets, who use misinformation (saying the wrong things about grace and faith) and disinformation (teaching half the truth and mixing doctrines up).

Example: It is wrong to teach that believers are still under the law, thereby undermining the finished work of Calvary by Jesus.

Watch!

1It is for freedom that Christ has set us free. Stand firm, then, and do not be encumbered once more by a yoke of slavery.

1 So Christ has truly set us free. Now make sure that you stay free, and don't get tied up again in slavery to the law.

2 Listen! I, Paul, tell you this: If you are counting on circumcision to make you right with God, then Christ will be of no benefit to you.

3 I'll say it again. If you are trying to find favor with God by being circumcised, you must obey every regulation in the whole law of Moses.

4 For if you are trying to make yourselves right with God by keeping the law, you have been cut off from Christ! You have fallen away from God's grace. (Gal.5:1-4, NLT)

Here, circumcision is a symbol of the flesh. It represents all those religious, cultural, traditional, social, personal, and national rules of engagement that men observe, thinking that they will deliver salvation to them. They will never deliver salvation to anyone as long as they are observed apart from the law of the Spirit of Life in Christ Jesus.

On the contrary, the law of the Spirit of Love in Christ, received through salvation and observed, delivers the eternal life we need apart from those tons of rules and regulations.
Don't take my word for it; let's ask the Holy Spirit:

19 the law applies to those to whom it was given, for its purpose is to keep people from having excuses, and to show that the entire world is guilty before God.
20 For no one can ever be made right with God by doing what the law commands. The law simply shows us how sinful we are.
21 But now God has shown us a way to be made right with him without keeping the requirements of the law, as was promised in the wrings of Moses and the prophets long ago.
22 We are made right with God by placing our faith in Jesus Christ. And this is true for everyone who believes, no matter who we are.
23 For everyone has sinned; we all fall short of God's glorious standard.

24 Yet God freely and graciously declares that we
are righteous. He did this through Christ Jesus
when he freed us from the penalty for our sins.
25 For God presented Jesus as the sacrifice for sin.
People are made right with God when they believe
that Jesus sacrificed his life, shedding his blood.
This sacrifice shows that God was being fair when
he held back and did not punish those who sinned
in times past,
26 for he was looking ahead and including them in
what he would do in this present me. God did this
to demonstrate his righteousness, for He himself is
fair and just, and he declares sinners to be right in
his sight when they believe in Jesus.
27 Can we boast, then, that we have done
anything to be accepted by God? No, because our
acquittal is not based on obeying the law. It is
based on faith.
28 So we are made right with God through faith
and not by obeying the law.
29 After all, is God the God of the Jews only? Isn't
he also the God of the Gentiles? Of course he is.

30 There is only one God, and he makes people right with himself only by faith, whether they are Jews or Gentiles.
31 Well then, if we emphasize faith, does this mean that we can forget about the law? Of course not! In fact, only when we have faith do we truly fulfill the law. (Rom3:19-31, NLT)

Let me quickly comment on the last verse (31), for those who will teach that we are still under the law based on misinterpretation of the verse.
Please observe and understand that he didn't say that when we have faith, we truly 'do' the law, but we truly 'fulfil' the law.

In other words, faith helps us to see and agree that "Christ is the end of the law" because He fulfilled them for us to be made free, indeed. Christ fulfilled the law, not we. Our part in the fulfilment is to believe that He did, and that what He did on the cross is enough to have fulfilled it. That's faith.

You don't have to go back to the dog's vomit in the mire.
We are free; only don't use your freedom as liberty to offend God and man again.

Walk in the Spirit, and you will not fulfil the lust of the flesh.

For in Jesus Christ neither circumcision availeth anything, nor uncircumcision; but faith which worketh by love. (Galaans 5:6,KJV)

For in Christ Jesus neither circumcision availeth anything, nor uncircumcision, but a new creature. (Galaans 6:15, KJV)

You can read it again and again in different Bible versions, until it sticks

On the other side of the coin, it is disinformation and misleading to teach that because we are no longer under the law, we can sin our way into freedom in the kingdom.

Scripture says you should re-examine yourself
to know if you are truly in faith.

Watch!

21 So just as sin ruled over all people and brought them to death, now God's wonderful grace rules instead, giving us right standing with God and

resulting in eternal life through Jesus Christ our Lord.

1 Well then, should we keep on sinning so that God can show us more and more of his wonderful grace?
2 Of course not! Since we have died to sin, how can we continue to live in it?
3 Or have you forgotten that when we were joined with Christ Jesus in baptism, we joined him in his death?
4 For we died and were buried with Christ by baptism. And just as Christ was raised from the dead by the glorious power of the Father, now we also may live new lives.—(Rom.5: 2021, 6:1-4, NLT)

Reading through the above, it is clear that anyone who purports to be a believer but continues in sin was not saved in the first place. For, according to the scripture, he is still alive to sin instead of being dead to it. If anyone is still alive to sin and living in it, this is proof enough that he was never saved in the first place.

If you have received salvation based on your inclination to sin,–whether you are alive or dead to sin,

– and the decisions you make about it, you cannot lose your salvation. This is because salvation is a gift that you did not earn through your own efforts initially.

The scripture says that God does not change His mind concerning His gift to His children. It is without repentance because the Holy Spirit that lives inside you would bear witness that you are saved and a child of God.

Watch!

For the gifts and calling of God are without repentance. (Romans 11:29, KJV)

Given the above background, let's answer the question of what the threats are to our relationship with God in salvation, especially in our contemporary times.

It has not changed. It is still the activities of the false prophets and fake teachers engaging in misinformation and disinformation that have come to be known as fake news.

Accordingly, these are the transporters or drivers of misinformation and disinformation, thus reducing and/or removing human interface, while others are consequences of human activities in abuse and self-seeking.

1. THE MEDIA (Social, Mainstream)
2. AI (Artificial Intelligence)
3. DRUGS AND SUBSTANCE ABUSE
4. CLIMATE CHANGE.
5. NUCLEAR ARMAMENT, WEAPONS OF MASS DESTRUCTION, CONFLICTS, INSECURITY, AND WARS

My objective is not to run an X-ray on each of the above existential threats to world peace, unity, and, above all, godliness. Those could be sourced online.

What is not in doubt is that these monsters, individually and jointly, have not only changed the face of the world in disorder but threatened the stability and unity of faith, stoking fear, doubt, and unbelief.

They are the horns that are scattering the world in general and targeting the church in particular.

Take, for instance, the Russia-Ukraine war. The destabilization it has caused on the world stage. Disruption in supply chains of virtually everything in the world, food and energy crises, regional conflicts, spiraling inflation, and financial and economic disruptions The massive use of weapons of mass killing and destruction, etc. The list goes on.

In the United States of America, no day passes without an incident of a mass shooting that kills people by the scores or hundreds, including children in primary and secondary schools.

These killings are carried out with assault weapons like the AR-15, amid constitutional debates and wrangling between Republicans and Democrats on the constitutional rights to carry guns and the need to wade in and institute common-sense gun controls as a check to the abuse.

Earthquakes, typhoon rains, hurricanes, floods, and wildfires, which are raging and wrecking everything and anything on their paths. These have devastated many parts of the world.

Political neocolonialism by the west against the African continent and the crushing effects of sit-tight regimes have refused to end, pushing the continent deeper into poverty, sickness, diseases, and political crisis, with coup d'état back on the stage and sweeping across the continent.

The 2019/2020 Coronavirus, which ravaged the whole world and crippled it for months, killing millions, is yet to be over, as there are indications of a resurgence in many parts of Asia.

The experts' view is that the last has not been heard of these strange disease-causing and crushing viruses, as man becomes desperate in the search for the unknown, only to stumble on his death.

Research into space, with men seeking another planet to escape to, has heightened.
This, to my mind, is another tower of Babel that will end in disaster. The earth is what the Lord has bequeathed to men to inhabit.

That's not surprising because Jesus hinted at each of these artifices as they were, as indicators of the beginning of the end.

Watch!

3 Later, Jesus sat on the Mount of Olives. His disciples came to him privately and said, "Tell us, when will all this happen? What sign will signal

your return and the end of the world? ” 4 Jesus
told them, “Don't let anyone mislead you,
5 for many will come in my name, claiming, 'I am
the Messiah.' They will deceive many.
6 And you will hear of wars and threats of wars,
but don't panic. Yes, these things must take place,
but the end won't follow immediately.
7 Nation will go to war against nation, and
kingdom against kingdom. There will be famines
and earthquakes in many parts of the world.
8 But all this is only the first of the birth pains, with
more to come.
9 “Then you will be arrested, persecuted, and
killed. You will be hated all over the world because
you are my followers.
10 And many will turn away from me and betray
and hate each other.
11 And many false prophets will appear and will
deceive many people.
12 Sin will be rampant everywhere, and the love
of many will grow cold.
13 But the one who endures to the end will be
saved.

14 And the Good News about the Kingdom will be preached throughout the whole world, so that all nations will hear it; and then the end will come. (Ma.24:3-14, NLT).

A close look with an eye of faith at the above scripture will reveal a serious alignment between where we are and where we are headed and what our Lord Jesus said, which cannot fall to the ground unaccomplished.

As a believer and an unbeliever alike, be wary of any teaching that points to oneself or the so-called miracles they have wrought, whether in ministry or business. All the offerings of what will end this or end that, cure this or cure that, resolve this or resolve that, bodily, spiritually, financially, in marriage, ministry, business, governance, and relationships, etc., are all part and parcel of the saying, "I am the Messiah," which Jesus has warned us about. In other words, people asserting themselves and what they do as solutions to the afflictions, sicknesses, diseases, hardships, discomforts, hunger, etc. their inventions, actions, and inactions have caused the world in the first place

Fear, anxiety, worry, greed, obsessions, self-esteem, and pride are all fertile grounds on which these deceptions fester and thrive. There are potholes that translate into pitfalls when we peevishly and sheepishly subscribe to them, only for them to swallow us like hell.

Maybe another scripture by the apostle whom Jesus specially hired would add value to the above.

Read 2 Tim 3:1-9 and 2 Peter 3. in any version of the Bible.

CHAPTER 17

PRAGMATIC RESPONSE TO THE THREATS

THE WAY OUT

I will be fooling you like the world does if I tell you that I have a solution to the world's problems and our share of them as believers, apart from what the Lord Himself revealed in His wisdom.

Did Jesus deceive us in John 16:33 when and where He said, In this world we would be persecuted, but in Him, we would have peace? He now commanded (not suggested) that we should rejoice or be of good courage because He had overcome the world. He followed this up in John 17, saying and praying to His Father to secure or shield us from the wicked one, because just as He was in the world but not of the world, we, His believers, are also in the world but not of the world. Why?

We are in Him, sing in heavenly places spiritually and positionally.
Are these statements true of you and what you believe? When Jesus made those profound declarations and apostolic prayers, He was in the world bodily. But

Certainly all his moons and emotions in utterances and teachings, especially at this point in me, were from start to finish heavenward. He was already looking beyond the cross, of which the world today is persecuting the believers. That's the unbeatable, undebatable solution to the temptation-ridden and ridiculed world of potholes.

This script is a wake-up call to the voice of the Holy Spirit.

Mortify therefore your members which are upon the earth; fornication, uncleanness, inordinate affection, evil concupiscence, and covetousness, which is idolatry: (Colossians 3:5, KJV).

What are you chasing in life?
To mortify means to discipline, to subject yourself to a certain goal, and to suppress. Literally, it means to die

to something-to sin the lust of the flesh, the lust of the eyes, and the pride of life.

Motivational speakers have charged believers to go for it, like the voice of the serpent in the garden to Eve, as though what we have and possess in this world will be a factor in deciding whether we will go to heaven or hell.

With all the advancement in science, technology, medicine, and inventions, which now litter every landscape of knowledge and dominate it, how come the world has become so Cainic and Hamic in satanic acquisions, duping and defrauding one another? Why are sicknesses and diseases on the increase—strange, resistant, daring, and malignant?

Show me one person who was buried with his material inheritances—houses, cars, money, etc.
Scripture says we should focus on the things above and not the things beneath.

Watch!

1. If ye then be risen with Christ, seek those things which are above, where Christ sitteth on the right hand of God.

2. Set your affection on things above, not on things on the earth.
3. For ye are dead, and your life is hid with Christ in God.
4. When Christ, who is our life, shall appear, then shall ye also appear with him in glory. (Col 3:1-4, KJV)

Don't get me wrong or mix it up. God is the God of prosperity and abundance. Heaven and earth and all the hosts, including the people that live there, are His and His alone. He bequeathed the earth to man to inherit in righteousness. It was man who handed control of his destiny to the devil through disobedience and is now baling with him to regain control. The earth is the Lord's and the fullness thereof.

Now, in mercy and love, that indiscretion has caused God, through His only-begotten Son, to restore us to God. Man, in his arrogance, is still debating his destiny with his Creator, chasing after creation instead of his Creator to inherit a better world prepared by God. Wealth without wisdom is wastage, not only of life on earth but of destiny hereafter.

Now, let's see how Jesus demonstrated this truth in our main text, taken from Mathew 24, which inspired the reference in the exhortation Apostle Paul gave above to the Church in Colosse.

Jesus was sing on Mount Olive. Mount Olive is located east of Jerusalem and is the highest peak in a ridge or table of mountains separated by a valley of Kidron.

It is so named because the sides are surrounded by olive trees. Olive trees bear olive fruits, from which olive oil is milled by crushing, beating, or being trodden by feet. This mountain, with a peak of 200 feet above the city ground, recorded many spiritual significances in the life and ministry of our Lord. It was here that he retired to devote himself privately to God, praying and meditating. Here he told the disciples the parable of the ten virgins, stood, and wept over Jerusalem.

Now he is sing on this mountain, telling them the highlights of how the present world would come to an end, as he told Noah when he wanted to destroy the first world.

It was from this mount that He ascended to heaven, and it is believed that He will step His feet on it when He returns to earth to fulfil the Davidic Covenant and eventually unveil the Kingdom of God.

Jesus was significantly above the world after suffering at the hands of the people. The ark of Noah was on top of the water of judgment when the first world was destroyed, and they were not allowed to disembark until the dove brought an olive leaf in its mouth to Noah. That was an indication of safety, life, prosperity, and posterity.

These virtues are metaphorically packaged in this sing position of Jesus (the highest peak of a mountain range, with a valley in between).

The surrounding environment (olive trees) is being spoken as a message into the lives of these disciples listening to Him, sharing secrets of the kingdom.

They were members of the privileged class who had renounced him until the end.

The point here is that you have to look beyond every mountain (power) in this world, all of which are jointly and severally below the Almighty power of God in Christ Jesus. Our help to escape the wrath of God is not in the mountains of this world, for by strength no one shall prevail. Our help comes from God. (Psalm 121)

As we look up to Jesus, knowing that we are seated with Him in heavenly places, though we are still in this world, we should keep in mind that we are surrounded by olive trees. Olives are usually crushed, beaten, trodden, and squeezed to mill out oil. Olive oil is known for its spiritual significance and for both healing and easing pain. So believers should understand that, as olive trees or fruits, we would be tried, tempted, and persecuted because of our faith in Jesus. Scripture says we should count it all joy (the oil of gladness) when we fall into diverse temptations. (James 1:1-8)

Jesus, by choice of a place to minister, its environment, dispositions (standing, sing, or walking), choice of words, me, and timing (examples cited), passes deep messages of salvation to those in inmate relationships with Him.

That was how I got the above revelations; I was neither taught them by any man nor read or heard them from anybody, but from the mouth of the Holy Spirit, my eternal teacher. I don't have the brains or smarts to conjure this revelation except through a gracious, inmate relationship with Jesus. To Him alone be the glory.

He told them they would be persecuted and even killed for His sake, which bespeaks of the beating and crushing of olive fruit to squeeze out the oil.

So rejoice, for great is your reward in heaven.

11. Blessed are ye, when men shall revile you, and persecute you, and shall say all manner of evil against you falsely, for my sake.
12. Rejoice, and be exceeding glad: for great is your reward in heaven: for so persecuted they the prophets which were before you. (Mathew 5:11–12, KJV)

Stay on top of the world, not with, against, or in it.
In another breath, the mountain could mean the church, with Jesus as the head. If God is for us, who can be against us?

When talking about staying on top of the world and not with, against, or in the world, it would be foolhardy not to acknowledge that we are living in the real world.

The family unit is the first block to building morality and character in children. This is complimented and strengthened by the church, schools, and community, each of which are formidable morality- and character-building institutions.

When you watch and listen to newsreels, programs, and activities on both social and mainstream media, it would not be difficult to gauge and read off, online in real me, the spiritual thermometer of the world. Its lightweight and featherweight categories in the boxing ring of the Word of God are not only alarming but frightening.

We shared in Chapter 13 the disingenuous act of Nmesoma Ejikeme, who insidiously forged her own result in the entrance examination to enter high school here in Nigeria. The pathetic dimension to that story that rocked the world was her boldness to do a video, telling the world that she was incapable of manipulating her own result on the website of the examination body, when in fact she did. She was deflated and devastated, and she came to her knees when she was confronted with the path she took to conceptualize, as it were, that crime.

QUESTIONS:

What role did the parents, teachers, church, and community play in either aiding or abetting this crime? Was she alone in carrying out the act?

Would all the building blocks spoken about feign ignorance that they did not see this coming, going by the character traits of Nmesoma?

There could be a thousand questions. The purpose here is not to apportion blame, pass the bulk, or even spite Nmesoma.

The point here is to draw attention to these building blocks and to know that the media and social media have become the Sodom and Gomorrah of our time, feeding the young ones in particular with destructive and satanic applications to self-destruct.

The entry of AI (artificial intelligence), advancing and galloping, will certainly complete the Samaritan hub that certainly needs divine visitation if we would get all the Zacheous of this world, short in morality and character, to the Sycamore tree of self-discipline to see from afar their salvation in Christ coming and within them to embrace. So help us, God.

CHAPTER 18

THE PARABOLIC TESTIMONIES OF THE NMESOMACHUKWUS

I have another story of another Nnesoma, this me not the one surnamed Ejikeme but Okonkwo, paraded on Arise TV on the 10th day of August, 2023, as the world's highest scorer in the 2023 UK Cambridge Exams. She beat all students in 145 countries to emerge as the best and brightest in the examination.

Nmesomachukwu, (spelt in full) as she was called and identified on that epic interview, probably to distinguish herself from the crime-tainted Mmesoma Ejikeme, recently paraded in the media for forging her entrance examination result, means favour or goodness.

I must say without fear of contradict on that both are really favoured by God. Notwithstanding the forbidden fruit, the later ate to tell us that light and darkness coexist. It's a matter of choice. Did you know that the tainted Nmesoma scored enough marks to fetch her admission in her chosen course of study?

But in pursuit of the prize money announced by a business tycoon in her town, she manipulated her score to surpass that of a kinswoman from the same state who had already been announced as the highest scorer.

Like Adam and Eve, she went for what she already had and lost everything because her score was withdrawn, and she was suspended from taking the exam for three years. Think about that; talk about being pennywise and pound foolish.

I don't blame the Okonkwo for stretching her own name to the full and quietly announcing to the whole world, "I am not that Egyptian rebel leader that took a sect of robbers to the wilderness," before she is cavilled and prosecuted in the people's court or parliament. To a mean mind, every Judas betrayed Christ; it was unknown to them that Judas and Jesus essentially meant the same thing but were separated by their works and tongues. Jesus is the Greek version of Jude, Judah, Joshua, Hoshea, or even Judas.

Nmesomachujwu Okonkwo is a student at Chrisland School in Victoria Garden City, Lekki, Lagos, Nigeria. She appeared on Arise TV, a cable network located in

Lagos, Nigeria, along with Mr. Timothy Jaiyeoba, a member of the school board.

You need to listen to this world champion. You wouldn't doubt for a minute that she deserved what her rang came up to—the best and the champ.

What got me thinking was what she said when they asked her what influenced and helped her performance.

She broke her answer into five distinct compartments.

What she did was show diligence in her studies by waking up very early in the wee hours of the night.
What her family did was support her by getting her all she needed, answering past questions, reducing her chores, etc.
What her school did was prepare them for school, keeping their eyes on the ball.
What her colleagues did was study together.
What her church did was, encourage and exhort all the way, emphasizing the need to distinguish themselves as children of God and tomorrow's leaders.

All these came together to launch her unto the world stage. She now stands tall, beaming with classic smiles, carrying the banner of victory so high.

Adding his voice to what Nmesomachukwu said, Mr. Jaiyeoba spoke about the vision and tenacity of the school in breeding world-class students like Nmesomachukwu that will rule the world in their chosen fields of studies, professions, and life engagements.

Founded in 1977, Chrisland is a centre for excellence, having been around for about 40 years and standing tall and stronger among equals. He posited that the performance of Nmesomachukwu was not a fluke or an accident. It's what they are known for, and there are many like her in their fold, adding that success requires engagement and empowerment. I agree. Who wouldn't seize such a golden opportunity for a cheap, minute-long ad? I wish the teacher, or a school board member, of the tainted Nmesoma could boldly face the Camera and tell the world what went wrong.

I now firmly believe that God has a reason for motivating me to renew my cable television subscription that I had neglected for months. I am convinced that it is precisely so I can tackle my God-given task of organizing my thoughts into books.

It was only the second day after that renewal when I sat in front of that TV to watch news, taking a break from my library and hours of laser focus on the screen of either my laptop and/or iPad-adapted phone, which are my word and literary kitchens, to cook ideas and manufacture literary foods inspirationally for the mind.

I have a daughter, the one and only one in the flesh. She is also called Nmesomachukwu Gold Okorie. Nmesoma, or Nmeso, for short, is our female Isaac and Obed and is worth more than seven sons to us.

In 2013, when she passed her high school exams at Methodist Girls High School in Lagos, Nigeria, she told me that she was not studying in our country, Nigeria. She gave two reasons that made her take that decision. One was that she was not prepared to spend a greater part of her life studying in school because of incessant strikes by university lecturers, which had become the norm rather than the exception. The second was that she was not prepared to be victimized and scandalized because she refused to sell her body for marks. I was touched. Not even my quiet and humble protest that I was in the twilight of my career could dissuade her.

Instead, she looked into my eyes and said, "God will provide". Do you think that was nebulous and flew in from the stratosphere? That was God's inspiration, surely. But how could she be inspired if she was not taught there is one called God, to whom we all owe everything in life?

Watch!

Direct your children onto the right path, and when they are older, they will not leave it. (Proverbs 22:6, NLT)

What is that enduring right path that is not le to the whims and caprices of mortal men to figure out? What a confused world that would be. In fact, that's where we are right now.

The two verses before that wise counsel in Proverbs taken together provides the answer to the question of what is or who is that right path (not paths) or way (not ways) which if taken by humanity will unify or redirect the world in thinking, actions and decision making.

4 True humility and fear of the LORD lead to riches, honor, and long life.
5 Corrupt people walk a thorny, treacherous road; whoever values life will avoid it.
6 Direct your children onto the right path, and when they are older, they will not leave it. (Pro. 22:4-6, NLT)

Let's do a quick number interpretation.

The number 4 in spirituality stands for stability (4 Cardinal Points: North, South, East, and West). That's the cross there. There, you see the Lord (Jesus) mentioned. The number 5 represents grace. We are saved by grace through faith. What is saved? Our souls, where you could see thorns and snares.

The number 6 stands for man. Man was created on the sixth day.
Man is now given instruction in this verse to train up the child in the way of Jesus. Get them to fear the Lord, get born again, and love God through Jesus. That way, they would be able, by grace through faith in Christ, avoid the thorns and snares that dot this wicked world and target the soul.

Yes, the devil will come after them, but because of the seed already planted in them, they will resist the devil, and the devil must flee.

Why?

4 But you belong to God, my dear children. You have already won a victory over those people, because the Spirit who lives in you is greater than the spirit who lives in the world.
5 Those people belong to this world, so they speak from the world's viewpoint, and the world listens to them.
6 But we belong to God, and those who know God listen to us. If they do not belong to God, they do not listen to us. That is how we know if someone has the Spirit of truth or the spirit of deception. (1 John 4:4-6, NLT)

Today, a 5- to 6-year-old child with a bold face would go to the parents and declare that it was a mistake that he or she came in the gender he or she came in, demanding that they be transgendered. Where do you think that voice is enabled and coming from?

Again, this me from the airwaves of the media—social, mainstream, print, and even contacts—sponsored by the devil, the prince of the air.

I was thinking that the essence of inventing a robust media technology that can control the airwaves was to challenge this wicked prince that took control of it. It's now clear to me how what is noble could be hijacked and plunged to the ground in unethical malfeasance.

I listened to an advertorial interlude on a popular cable TV show where a popular Nollywood star said that art media is a powerful tool and platform to explore and express what you want. Absolutely!

What you want is not what is right. It's all about what you want; it doesn't matter if it is reprehensible or not, and that's why it's a star punch aired intermittently minutes before the commencement of any program on that cable network.

It didn't start today. That was exactly how the first deception was conceptualized, packaged as a lie, and transported into the heart of man to cause the worst cancerous damage to his soul in generations.

The strategy has not changed but has become modular, encrypted, and digitized.

Artificial intelligence, riding and flying on the wings of social media and the Internet, is fast taking over the minds and hearts of the world, especially the spongy, mind-narrated children, and fast producing not tech giants in ingenuity but impudent giants in immorality and decadence (children and adults alike) with gaping character deficits.

The family, community, especially the faith community, and institutions of basic and high learning, which appear to be the breeding centres for experimenting on these demonic spirits, must not keep quiet to make the virtual channels active and energetic. Governments at every level in every nation must rise up against this incredulous evil in our time.

Watch around and see what drugs are doing to this generation, turning humans into zombies. We are losing our siblings to the wicked world, which has opened the forest of fruits of the knowledge of good and evil for all to pluck, eat, and see that the devil tastes good and pleasurable. They campaign openly. It is unknown to them that there is death in the pot.

Nakedness, fear, shame, vulnerability, unproductivity across the board, and even death in a wasted generation are usually the end products. As it was in the beginning, so it is, and so shall it be, world without end.

They will tell you how free they are to live the life they have chosen without wisdom, but they will never tell you how ensnared and bound they are. Perhaps they do not know they are in bondage. Like Adam and Eve, they will be hiding and evading the light spotlighting them, and unfortunately, they will plunge to death in destruction.

This is not a sudden thing; the scriptures warn us about these end-me manifestations and posit that they should cease.

We will be making mistakes by thinking that we can write, teach, shout, and pray our way out of these perilous times.

We need to add actions to these seemingly passive responses because an urgent threat, even a storm, needs an urgent reaction—flee. Let's run to God as fast as we can.

Watch this year's 2023 Women's World Cup finals in Australia. You can't, as we speak, distinguish between them and their male counterparts playing in the men's version. The same thing is happening in the boxing ring.

My point is about cultural wars and superiority complexes. Women want to become and do what men do, and men want to become women in a cultural war and identity crisis. The dynamics of sin in origin and methodology are "boundary crossing" in violation of spiritual, natural, international, institutional, cultural, social, organizational, and even parental laws.

I am not about to vent on laws in any form or shape here.

Believers are not under the law, just as we are not without a law. Scripture says laws are made and meant for the lawless. In Christ Jesus, we are indeed made free to become the face of grace in obedience, living above the law. To whom much is given, much is expected.

The harmless law of origin has remained the one and only law: "Don't disobey your creator."

Did you know that the first digitized and encrypted Internet was, that's right, "The Word of God," the Bible?

This is not because, in written form as the book of books, it's the most widely published, circulated, and read book, but because "When God spoke to Adam, He spoke to the whole world" that was unfolding through him. The unborn generations in his loins in eternity heard that. That's how loud and dominant the voice of God could be. This is true of all creations, which is why, when man (Adam) sinned, all sinned, since all came out of the same man.

That blood tainted with sin thus entered every human born of a woman, multiplied, and spread, such that no one can say that he has no sin. (1John1:9. Rom3:23)

The only me sin was bridged sustainably, just as you can bridge electric current to stop its transmission by introducing a conductor, was when Jesus was to manifest in the flesh.

The power of God came upon the Virgin Mary, and the Holy Spirit overshadowed her to protect that divine gene that embodied the supernaturally introduced egg into her womb. No man met Mary.

I checked the dictionary meaning of the word 'overshadow', and here is what I found:

- (*transitive*) To obscure something by casting a shadow.
- (*transitive*) To dominate something and make it seem insignificant.

- (*transitive*) To shelter or protect.

You see, Mary was just a mere vessel God used to birth the miracle of the entry into the world of His Son, Jesus.

God does not need any permission to do what He wants to do; He is sovereign. But he would not break the law, but could suspend it to carry out a sovereign will in wisdom.

The significance of this revelation is to show that it takes God's supernatural intervention to stop sin, not effort, morality, or character, all of which would be enabled through the encrypted blood of Jesus embodying them all.

When any man confesses his sin to God and accepts His Son Jesus Christ as his Saviour, he is forgiven of his sin and washed by that encrypted blood, carrying the life of God—not just a more abundant life but eternal life.

The disc of a computer comes with all the coded commands incorporated: lettering, voice, picture image, print, forward, store, retrieve, etc.

The blood of Jesus carries the life of God, and the life of God in Christ carries the word, wisdom, wishes, works, and wonders of God in man. Receive it. (Lev 17:11) Back to my daughter, Nmesoma, because I did not forget.

With the active support of my wife and a family friend, Mrs. Felicitas Momoh, who was working in a subsidiary of my workplace and was pushing the same agenda for their beloved daughter Elizabeth, we collaborated, prayed, and pushed until these two girls, with the help of God, got through and travelled to the United States of America on the 1st of August 2014 to study, having passed the required entrance exams and getting their visas by divine orchestration.

That day happened to be my beloved daughter's birthday.

I recall that a friend of mine, indeed a close brother and second cousin, called me wicked, telling me that my wife and I had hearts for sending our only daughter abroad to study. Though I owed nobody, including him, an apology and was not going to seek anyone's permission or help, as help comes from God, I took me to explain to him that it was neither my idea nor my decision as such. But I saw God in it, all the same.

Today, his own children are doing Master's degrees in the United Kingdom, for which I give God glory, especially since He has made it crime-free for parents to send their children abroad to study, except for those with only one kid.

Another cousin of mine, with a bold face, went to my senior sister (unfortunately late now) and insidiously asked her, How would I now cope since I was out of work, just one month after my daughter travelled abroad to study, with all the financial implications?

My senior sister's answer to her was: "Don't you know Chinkere (me)? He wouldn't take such a major step without a plan". She was right. But it's not even about my plan, but my plan in God, which no man can uproot when it is deep enough and done in faith.

Nmesoma, Chinazaekpere Okorie, as we speak, is working in a Fortune 500 financial company after her Master's degrees in business analytics.

Her first degree was in information technology. Her sister friend, Elizabeth, is on the verge of completing her second degree too in the medical field, which takes a longer period of me after her first degree in chemistry.

Gold said with her own mouth, "God would provide," like the answer Abraham gave to Isaac when he initially asked him, "Where is the lamb that is going to be used for the sacrifice, since he could see the wood and the fire, which incidentally he was carrying? Sometimes you could be carrying what seems to be death, but the end thereof is life, if God puts it on you. The opposite is also true.

Only God can do this for those who look up to Him for succour and support. To Him alone be the glory.

On this, I pay tribute to Mr. and Mrs. Laval, a relative of Mr. and Mrs. Momoh, who provided a launch pad from where those children took off to their school in 2014 and sheltered them each me they were on break. Truly, (Nwanne di na mba). A friend in need is indeed a friend. May your own children break the record.

Recall, as I shared in my flagship, SUCCESS MINDSET, blazing the trail in my formal authorship, that it was in September 2014, the same year, that I exited my workplace in early retirement, just one month after my daughter travelled.

How then was this finance-centric and exchange-upsetting project of financing a foreign currency-domiciled education undertaken?

Not possible without God. My untraceable role and path with my wife in covenant relationship with God, of course, and Nmesoma as part of it, will drop very soon in another finance management and covenant-keeping project to encourage others.

When, in obedience, you bring the wood and fire of prayer, the lamb will be provided by faith for a bloody sacrifice unto praise.

Success has no ancient formula in print. It answers to obedience and sacrifice. The wood and fire come from men; the lamb and altar come from God. When they meet, life is saved, and prosperity is inevitable.

Shalom.

CHAPTER 19

REVELATORY PERSPECTIVES AND EXHORTATIONS

My general take on this discourse is that Shem is not different from Japhet in pursuit of earthly blessings through clean and godly wisdom.

There is hardly anywhere in the world where you would not see Jews, blessed as they are, acquiring, building, and thriving, especially in the Jewish world. That is connected to this exceptional blessing of God on them.

However, Jesus, the source of that wisdom and wealth, would rule over both in a tent called the church, which will translate to the Kingdom of God, with Him as the King. Recall that Jesus sat on that mount (the church of gracious power) as the head, towering over every mount.

I do not share the school of thought that tries to explicate this deep spiritual prophecy, looking at the wars that saw some heathens (Greece, Rome, etc.) conquer and occupy Israel, which wars were ephemeral in nature. At best, it could be the natural dimension of that prophecy, carried out in envy. Seen differently, that's the crushing and treshing of the olive fruits to squeeze out the oil.

Blessings provoke envy in some, especially in those of brotherly descent. The ants swarm around the sugary cake, and the rats appear when the cheese is put on the table.

Accordingly, the church, being the union of the Jews (Shem) and Gentiles (Japhet), is also the house of true wealth and an acceptable profession of good religion. Through prosperity, the gospel spreads abroad. That's ongoing.

The curse on Canaan is not a sentence to hell but a lower ranking relative to others. After all, scripture says it is better to be a gatekeeper in the house or tent of God than take residence in the house or place of the wicked.

The prodigal gathered himself, recovered himself from prodigality, and retraced his steps. When he did, he was accepted and celebrated. Wisdom begins when you accept, in humility, where God has placed you in life, for in due course you will reap promotion if you are faithful to the small commitments made to you.

In the interim, the curse, as it were, has been fulfilled in two ways.

a) Naturally and physically: Israel made most of the children of Ham, the Canaanites, their servants (hewers of wood and fetchers of water) when, in about 1250 BC, they conquered Canaan and drove them out of that promised land. Believe it or not, some of them became proselytizing Jews.

b) Spiritually and heavenly speaking: Jesus Christ, the descendant of Shem, has died on the cross to redeem the whole world, founded and established the church in Jerusalem, sent the Holy Ghost to empower the church, and the gospel gate is open, the preaching of which has spread abroad, from Jerusalem to Judea to Samaria and right into the uttermost parts of the world. Apostles Peter and Paul have championed the spread of the gospel to many parts of Europe and Asia, and up to date, the kingdom of God is spreading and prospering even through the wealth of the gentiles, and the kingdom of hell cannot prevail against it.

Jesus, not man, is truly building His church and has made all things beautiful in His own me.

Hallelujah!

The descendants of Ham, wherever they are, are, by grace through faith in Jesus, welcomed into the Church, the tent into which the whole world is united in Christ.

There is no pothole-free world, spotless person, or church under the sun.
Hear this and hear it loud and clear as the biggest takeaway from this project commissioned by the Lord and why He so did for our learning.

As long as this earth remains, whether you are Semitic, Hamitic, or Japhetic within the context of this discourse, no one is blameless. All have spots or pitfalls and are full of potholes that need to be cleansed and closed. Most of these pitfalls are not even obvious to our knowledge and understanding. (Rom.3:23). We only know in part.

The believer and the church that he has fled to are not fully redeemed; they are in a world full of hamitic spirits and the enemies of the church. This is the natural man that would persecute and hound believers because of ignorance, as was foretold and declared in the scriptures.

But Jesus says we should rejoice and know that He is the captain of the ship sailing to a safe harbor. His death on the cross abolished every dichotomy in the world and united it in Him.

Don't just take my word for it; the infallible word of God is our backbone. For he is our peace, who hath made both one, and hath broken down the middle wall of partition between us; (Ephesians 2:14, KJV).

23. Before the way of faith in Christ was available to us, we were placed under guard by the law. We were kept in protective custody, so to speak, until the way of faith was revealed.
24. Let me put it another way. The law was our guardian until Christ came; it protected us until we could be made right with God through faith.
25. And now that the way of faith has come, we no longer need the law as our guardian.
26. For you are all children of God through faith in Christ Jesus.
27. And all who have been united with Christ in baptism have put on Christ, like putting on new clothes.
28. There is no longer Jew or Gentile, slave or free, male and female. For you are all one in Christ Jesus.

29. And now that you belong to Christ, you are the true children of Abraham. You are his heirs, and God's promise to Abraham belongs to you. (Galatians 3:23-29, NLT).

This being one in Christ, such that there is no longer male or female, does not abolish the differences between a natural man and a female. Hiding under it to justify the satanic and demonic transgender project being sponsored by the devil is an abuse of scripture in unrighteous interpretation. Boundaries still exist and must be respected. It is only in matters of faith and our privileges in Christ that those boundaries, as middle walls of partition, have been broken.

15. Christ is the visible image of the invisible God. He existed before anything was created and is supreme overall creation,
16. for through him God created everything in the heavenly realms and on earth. He made the things we can see and the things we can't see—such as thrones, kingdoms, rulers, and authorities in the unseen world. Everything was created through him and for him.
17. He existed before anything else, and he holds all creation together.

18. Christ is also the head of the church, which is his body. He is the beginning, supreme over all who rise from the dead. So he is first in everything.
19. For God in all his fullness was pleased to live in Christ,
20. and through him God reconciled everything to himself. He made peace with everything in heaven and on earth by means of Christ's blood on the cross.
21. This includes you who were once far away from God. You were his enemies, separated from him by your evil thoughts and actions.
22. Yet now he has reconciled you to himself through the death of Christ in his physical body. As a result, he has brought you into his own presence, and you are holy and blameless as you stand before him without a single fault.
23. But you must continue to believe this truth and stand firmly in it. Don't drift away from the assurance you received when you heard the Good News. The Good News has been preached all over the world, and I, Paul, have been appointed as God's servant to proclaim it. (Colossians 1:15-23, NLT.)

You see, it's now a level playing field for all to play by faith. The law finished its work of showing man his true state in sin, which was its purpose. Then God revealed the solution to sin, which is by grace through faith in His Son.

Whether you are a Jew, a Gentile, a male or a female, a slave or free, foolish or wise, once you come to Jesus and receive His Spirit, you are saved and blessed with the blessing of Abraham, the father of faith.

Therefore it is of faith, that it might be by grace; to the end the promise might be sure to all the seed; not to that only which is of the law, but to that also which is of the faith of Abraham; who is the father of us all, (Rom 4:16, KJV)

If Noah and everybody in the ark, under a now-defunct covenant, made it, floating on the water of judgment for about five months, how would the Son of God, Who made the supreme sacrifice of death on the cross, not deliver us safe and sound into the presence of His Father in the Kingdom, that He is the King?

Impossicant! According to my people in this double-sword vocabulary

We all need the Saviour for total salvation. The only one who is spotless, pothole-free, and has the answer to every issue of life is our Lord Jesus Christ, who has promised to build His church, not any man under the sun.
Believers are mere labourers, hired at various times to build and occupy until He comes to pay the wages, as illustrated in the parable of the vineyard (see Ma 9:38; 20:1–16).

Jesus has the master plan of the church and is the chief cornerstone. In fact, He is the Saviour and the Redeemer of our souls, torn by wounds sustained in the race of this life, and to find rest in the grace of God. In Him and with Him, there is no Japheth, Ham, or Shem.

We are all united as one in love for God, to escape the wrath of God in judgment like that which saved Noah and his family. Those that will reject Him as their Lord should know, for certain, that they cannot pay for their sins because salvation is not priced in any human currency and is not available on the shelves of shopping malls in Dubai, UAE, Quarter, UK, USA, Germany, and/or France, etc. It is unaffordable to man, costlier, and beyond the total wealth of this world.

Your gorgeous and beautiful buildings, families, education, possessions, positions and placements, titles and earthly crowns, governments, intellectual property, spirituality without Christ, etc. cannot save you beyond (Eber) and cross you over (Heber) this world.

As in the flood, they would all perish and be consumed by God's fire of judgment, along with Satan, who would also be judged for conspiring with the kings of earth and false prophets.

You need to shoot (salah) beyond here on earth, in the midst of this failing and passing world, in order to separate (peleg) yourself from the destruction that is coming upon it and to pave the way for eternal inheritance in Christ Jesus.

CHAPTER 20

ONLY JESUS CAN SAVE A MAN FROM POTHOLES AND DELIVER HIM INTO POTHOLE-FREE WORLD

I have told you all this so that you may have peace in me. Here on earth you will have many trials and sorrows. But take heart, because I have overcome the world. (John 16:33, NLT)

Probing further in pursuit of this divine agenda, let's engage on a friendly note:

What is your attitude toward your parents, employers, teachers, elders, pastors, etc., and those placed in authority over you?

Is it any wonder that God made the honouring of our parents the first commandment under heaven and the fourth in general, and the only commandment with benefits of longevity attached?

It may be argued that Ham's father did not curse him directly. I believe this was because God had already blessed all of them in chapter 9.

Noah had a good understanding of divine principles and order and knew he could not curse those whom God had blessed.

He went straight for and against the last son of Ham, Canaan, who may have manifested the same impunity as his father in character.
But remember, under the law, a curse on one could be a curse for all. When the leader failed, all failed and were sanctioned. That's how I, you, and the whole world inherited the sin of Adam and Eve.

Though the descendants of Ham were energetic and the most advanced in primitive Babylonian history, inventing, creating a literary world, wring many books, and building cities and kingdoms to showcase their prowess, they were later conquered on all fronts by the Celtic and Semitic races. They therefore could not excel. That's the point. It is Reubenistic; thou shalt not excel, Jacob declared.

It is characteristic of man to thrive in the flesh and crash soon afterwards.

The flesh is fragile and unsustainable in a sobering state after some crazy engagements. Remember the events of the Garden of Eden? "You are le reeling in wounds after damage has been done."

Did you know that your possessions and position in this world in terms of material acquisitions and possessions are not evidence that you are either blessed or cursed? They could be deceptive either way.

Both curses and true blessings are not outward in identity and expression but inward in knowledge and awareness. It's not about who you are or claim to be, but who you are and choose to obey.

The scripture provides some inspirational guidelines in these regards.

1. Blessed *is* the man that walketh not in the counsel of the ungodly, nor standeth in the way of sinners, nor sitteth in the seat of the scornful.

2. But his delight *is* in the law of the LORD; and in his law doth he meditate day and night.

3. And he shall be like a tree planted by the rivers of water, that bringeth forth his fruit in his season; his leaf also shall not wither; and whatsoever he doeth shall prosper.
4. The ungodly *are* not so: but *are* like the chaff which the wind driveth away.
5. Therefore the ungodly shall not stand in the judgment, nor sinners in the congregation of the righteous.
6. For the LORD knoweth the way of the righteous: but the way of the ungodly shall perish. (Psalms 1:1-6, KJV)

7. This book of the law shall not depart out of thy mouth; but thou shalt meditate therein day and night, that thou mayest observe to do according to all that is written therein: for then thou shalt make thy way prosperous, and then thou shalt have good success. 9.
Have not I commanded thee? Be strong and of a good courage; be not afraid, neither be thou dismayed: for the LORD thy God is with thee whithersoever thou goest. (Jos 1:8-9, KJV)

Jesus agrees and confirms.

39. And she had a sister called Mary, which also sat
at Jesus' feet, and heard his word.
40. But Martha was cumbered about much serving,
and came to him, and said, Lord, dost thou not care
that my sister hath le me to serve alone? bid her
therefore that she help me.
41. And Jesus answered and said unto her, Martha,
Martha, thou art careful and troubled about many
things:
42. But one thing is needful: and Mary hath chosen
that good part, which shall not be taken away from
her. (Luke 10:39-42, KJV)

TESTIMONY

Recall the investment I made in 2012, which eleven years later did not materialize?

Just two weeks after that message, which I was inspired to write to the secretary of the sponsors and promoters of that investment, I took delivery of the investment as the Holy Spirit put fire on their comfort of absurdity.

Though everything about the investment revealed Japhetic spirit in conception and layout, it is one of those hamitic executions I have ever seen in my lifetime. The massive fraud that took place there and delayed its speedy execution, completion, and allocation within two years as promised in their brochure is not only evident but endemic and damning.

This is a reflection of what goes on in many homes, groups, societies, and governments, even in the body of Christ.
Blood touching blood in massive frauds of unprecedented dimensions

Material poverty is a joke compared to a defective soul lacking in good conscience.

What I saw, in no small measure, reflected the satanic character, decadence, and bankruptcy of the minds of those who had anything to do with that project. The stamp of emblematic shame, like a stench reaching the high heavens, which are curse-worthy, is unmistakable as you walk around the project.
"By their fruits, you will know them".

Most of the people behind those projects, like our political leaders who travel abroad, know the standards and quality they meet overseas. But they come back home and deliver poor-quality jobs at the most expensive cost to the people. It is a tale of woe that has undermined the credibility of African nations. The worst is that some of the people behind these frauds are "believers", who probably think that the God of heaven, who created the eyes, does not see them. It's for this reason that many undergo strange things in their lives, because the wicked do not know where they stumble.

May God have mercy on Ham and his descendants, who populated Africa with Mizraim and Lud (see our family tree in Fig. 1). Amen
Our escape is only in Christ, not in acquision through stealing, killing, and destruction.

WARNING:

DON'T BRING CURSES ON YOURSELF OR YOUR HOUSEHOLD BY LIES, LOOTING, OR
EMBEZZLEMENT OF PUBLIC FUNDS. IF YOU DO, YOUR SIN MUST CERTAINLY FIND YOU OUT. PROBITY IS A VIRTUE—FEAR GOD.

In closing and fixing the pothole of sin in our lives, Jesus preached a great message on the mount.

The summary of the highlights of those beatitudes and the doctrines that follow is that in Him, they are all jointly and severally fulfilled.
Consequently, anyone in Him would rather than fill his head with the notions of those requirements, have his spirit and soul empowered to live a victorious life.

The Holy Spirit, which is His Spirit that abides in and with us, prepares us to enjoy life in the sprawling and expansive Kingdom of God in Christ, just ahead of Eber, beyond this world, Heber, and passing over it to Celebrate.

It is obvious from all the foregoing discourse that the twelve patriarchs of Israel are far better than the twelve princes of the nations. The dwelling places of the noble on earth could be palacious, but the tents of the saints are homes and preferred because in the tent of Shem (not the palaces of Ham or even the fortresses of Japhet), God dwells to abide and bless.

There is yet one point in my mind that I don't want buried in the rubble of this presentation and lost.

It was on the track of the pronouncement of a mortal man called Noah that the world has been reeling, running, rolling, and evolving towards the end of the Kingdom of God, now perfected and vested in Jesus

Christ, the Holy One of Israel, that has the final judgment. Ethnological science and history are witnesses to this truth.

God Almighty honored the words of a man who, by His Word, was the only righteous man in his me.

Did you observe that God did not a ach any material references or achievements to Noah that influenced His acceptance and categorization of him or the status He conferred on him as His righteous?

Heirship of faith was delivered to him before any and pushed his profile to the status of a faith hero in the hall of fame of faithful men.

His spiritual pedigree could be measured by the spontaneous response he gave to every command God gave him. "And Noah did exactly as God commanded him", a complementary commentary in recognion you see in God's dealings with his servants like Moses to emphasize obedience from the heart with dispatch as a faithful requirement to make a success of the charter of faith with Him.

A man who spent one hundred and fifty years constructing an ark according to the command of God without wavering and another 150 days boxed in that ark, floating on the risky water of judgment, is, by every dint of assessment, a man at rest with God. Earthly wealth can't buy that.

It is no surprise that God honored his word as a precursor to what His Son, Jesus, would inherit and finished up on Calvary through His death and resurrection as the last man anchoring this sprawling race of grace.

I doff my hat to Noah, a faith hero by every standard (Heb. 11:7), but bow my knees to Jesus, his creator and enabler.

In this regard, I submit that greatness is achieved through goodness in obedience to God. And there is only one who is good enough to have offered an acceptable sacrifice of His good life to atone for the sins of the whole world and deliver His goodness to us.

It is only by Him and through Him that anyone, whether Semitic, Hamitic, or Japhetic, in any part of the earth or even another planet would receive forgiveness of sin and escape the wrath of God's judgment. All have been united and invited to receive Jesus Christ as the Messiah to save them from their sins. Those who respond and believe are called believers, while those who reject Jesus Christ are unbelievers. Believers and unbelievers are therefore the two categories of people on earth today. It is no longer Shem, Ham, and Japheth that will face the judgment of God, to be presided over by His Son, Jesus, at the end of this world.

If you have received Jesus as your Lord and Saviour, you are Hebrew by right and entitled to the blessings of Abraham by grace through faith and looking beyond.

Happy, then, are you?

If otherwise, you still have the opportunity (but not the time) to make peace with your creator now by confessing and receiving Jesus as your Lord and Saviour.

Please head to: "faith dedication page" at the end of this chapter to dedicate your life to Him and secure it eternally. We will be sharing contacts to reach you and relate more with you.

My book titled "Partake and Connect to God: The Power of Holy Communion" is helpful in this regard.
It is available in major bookshops and as an e-book.
Shalom.

More of Him, and blessed are you in God's speed!

DEDICATION OF ONE'S LIFE TO CHRIST

Father, thank You for sending Your Son
Jesus Christ to die and pay for my sins. I
receive Him as My Lord And Saviour.
I believe He rose again from the dead to deliver Your
Life to me, which I now believe and receive.
Thank You Jesus, Come and live in me.
I am a new creation. Amen.

OTHER BOOKS BY THE AUTHOR

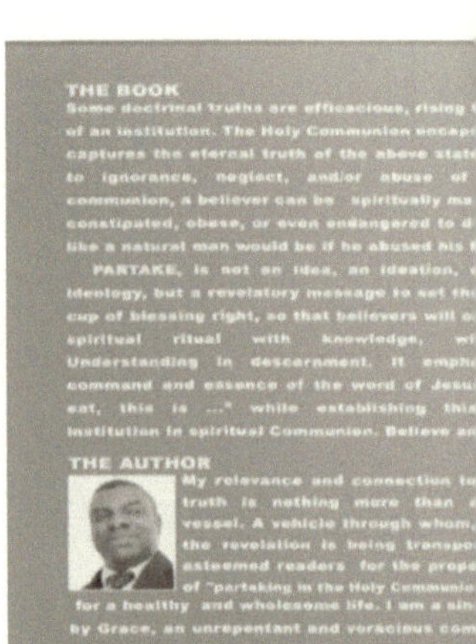

www.ingramcontent.com/pod-product-compliance
Lightning Source LLC
LaVergne TN
LVHW041156150826
845673LV00001B/176

* 9 7 8 9 7 8 7 8 1 9 6 1 6 *